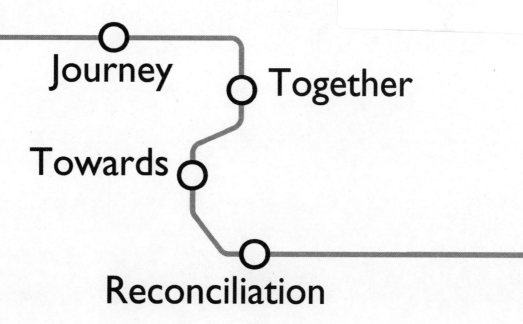

Journey Together Towards Reconciliation

Resources for catechists accompanying parents
of children preparing to celebrate Reconciliation

PADDY RYLANDS

Kevin
Mayhew

First published in 2000 by
KEVIN MAYHEW LTD
Buxhall, Stowmarket,
Suffolk IP14 3BW

ISBN 1 84003 609 5
Catalogue No 1500381

0 1 2 3 4 5 6 7 8 9

Cover design by Jonathan Stroulger
Edited by Helen Elliot
Typesetting by Louise Selfe
Printed in Great Britain

About the Author

For twenty years Paddy Rylands has worked with catechists involved in sacramental preparation, first of all in the parish of Our Lady and St Joseph, Hanwell, and for the past fourteen years as a member of Shrewsbury Diocese Education Service where she is advisor for parish and adult formation.

Foreword

It is good to be able to recommend this publication. Its aim is to offer practical help in addressing the important role of parents and parish in the preparation of our children for the Sacraments, and its starting point is the recognition that all of us need to grow in appreciation of these Sacraments. They are gifts of God to his people, inviting us and enabling us to enter more fully into the Paschal Mystery of Jesus. Responding is a life-long affair. One of the many strengths of this book is that it sees the time of First Celebration of the Sacrament as an opportunity for all concerned to deepen that response. Material to enable catechists and parents to do so forms the main content of these pages.

What we are given, however, is not so much a programme to be worked through as a process with which to operate. Given that all of us are at different stages in understanding and responding to the Sacraments, the emphasis here is on discovering what material is appropriate for both catechists and parents. A variety of resources are made available but the need for adaptation to meet specific needs is constantly urged. There is no alternative but to meet people where they are and to start from there. What is important is that appropriate help is available to take the next step forward in understanding and response.

It is impossible to read this book and not realise that it comes from the pen of a 'hands on' practitioner. Heeding its advice and its eye for detail in planning will ensure that many a pitfall is avoided. I recommend it and hope it will be used widely.

Brian M. Noble
Bishop of Shrewsbury
June, 2000

For Lena
and in memory of Joseph
who first taught our family the reality of reconciliation.

With grateful thanks and appreciation:

to the many people whose support and practical help have made this book possible;

to Bernard Bickers, Catherine Darby SND, Michael Winstanley SDB, Rosemary McCloskey and June Edwards who prepared resources for this book;

and with immeasurable thanks to Rowena Nield for her painstaking typing, preparation and proof-reading of the manuscript.

Contents _____

PART 1. Guidelines for Catechists

PART 2. Resources for Reconciliation

PART 1
Guidelines for Catechists

Remember that we are listened to with much greater satisfaction when we ourselves are enjoying our work; for what we say is affected by the very joy of which we ourselves are aware, and it proceeds from us with greater ease and with more acceptance . . . The important thing is that everyone should enjoy catechising; for the better we succeed in this the more attractive we shall be.

The rule which is to be our guide is not difficult to find. For if in material matters God loves a cheerful giver (1 Corinthians 9:7), how much more will he in spiritual matters? But the certainty that this joy will be with us at the right time is something that depends on the mercy of the one who has given us this teaching.

St Augustine on 'Catechising the Uninstructed' in Jean Comby, *How to Read Church History*, volume 1.

Using these Resources

1. Working with Parents

These resources are planned for use with parents of children preparing to celebrate the Sacrament of Reconciliation. It is anticipated that they

- form but one part of the parish's overall provision of adult catechesis and are organised in the light of this
- take into account what the parish offers to parents both *before* and *after* preparation for this Sacrament
- reflect an awareness of the way school and parish work in partnership.

They are intended for *adaptation*.

To be used most appropriately, it is presumed that the catechist

- knows her/his parents, their questions and concerns, their experience of adult catechesis, of group work
- is 'at home' with the theme and familiar with the relevant scripture passages, Church traditions and teachings
- is familiar with the catechetical process on which the material is based, that is:
    a. inviting participants to name and then reflect on their personal experience of the particular theme
    b. offering appropriate 'input', sharing the Church's teachings/traditions
    c. allowing time for further reflection leading towards an integration of what has been shared into the lives of participants
    d. celebrating.

(This way of working is described as the 'Pastoral Cycle'. A more detailed explanation is given on page 28.)

For each session, material is offered from which the catechist can make a selection so that the needs and situations of the particular group of parents are truly met. If the catechist is to accompany others on their faith journey, the starting point is the reality of *their* lives – the journey begins with the parents.

There is a variety of ways of working with parents as they prepare to celebrate sacraments:

- on an individual basis
- in small-group clusters
- as a large group, meeting in either the school or parish hall.

These resources are prepared for the larger group meeting, but can be easily adapted to use either with smaller groups or as points for discussion with individual families.

They are intended for *adaptation*.

2. Accompanying Parents as their children prepare to celebrate sacraments

These resources have been prepared on the understanding that

- parents, in general, want the best and will do their best for their children
- school, parish and family can be powerful influences on children growing in faith, particularly when they work in partnership
- a child's time of preparation for sacraments is a 'ripe' occasion to offer to parents an invitation to participate in a programme of adult catechesis
- adults have *the right* to catechesis (*Catechesi Tradendae,* para. 64, Catholic Truth Society, 1979)
- many adults appreciate the opportunity: to reflect on their faith with others, to share their questions and concerns, to update themselves with the tradition and teachings of the Church
- parents enjoy, as well as find helpful, the opportunity to discuss with other parents ways of sharing faith with their children.

The role of parents as catechists of their children is considered to be of great importance in the Church:

> It goes without saying that Christian parents are the primary and irreplaceable catechists of their children.
>
> *Christifideles Laici,* para. 34
> Catholic Truth Society, 1988

In Pope John Paul II's address to the parents of First Communicants at Cardiff, he emphasises their vital part in bringing up their children 'in the ways of faith':

> Dear parents of these children: your love for Christ has made this day possible. For you are your children's first teachers in the ways of faith. By what you say and do, you show them the truths of our faith and the values of the Gospel. This is indeed not only a sacred duty, but a grace, a great privilege. Many other members of the Church share in this task, but the main responsibility for your children's religious formation rests upon your shoulders. So try to make your homes genuinely Christian. Help your children to grow and mature as Jesus did at Nazareth, 'in wisdom, in stature and in favour with God and men' (Luke 2:52). Allow no one to take advantage of their lack of experience and knowledge. As you share with them in their personal pilgrimage to God, may you always be united in prayer and worship and in humble love of God and his people.
>
> *The Pope Teaches – The Pope in Britain*
> Catholic Truth Society, 1982

But it is not just children who benefit:

> The parents themselves profit from the effort that this demands of them, for in a catechetical dialogue of this sort, each individual both receives and gives.
>
> *Catechesi Tradendae,* para. 68
> Catholic Truth Society, 1979

The question, 'Who supports and catechises the parents?' needs to be addressed. If it is accepted

- that catechesis is the 'right of all believers' (*Catechesi Tradendae,* para. 64)
- that the parish is the 'pre-eminent place for catechesis' (*Catechesi Tradendae,* para. 67)
- that adult catechesis is the 'principal form' (*Catechesi Tradendae,* para. 43)

then those involved in leadership in the parish are called to give serious consideration and reflection to the catechesis being offered to adults, especially to parents with children preparing to celebrate sacraments.

You might find it helpful to read:

'Congregation for the Clergy', *General Directory for Catechesis,* Catholic Truth Society, 1997

3. Offering Catechesis to Adults in the Parish – some possibilities

(This outline is based on a vision of inviting parishioners to participate in catechesis on a number of occasions during their lifelong journey in faith – either individually, in small groups, in family clusters or in larger groups within the community setting.)

When preparing to celebrate sacraments

For adults as parents, sponsors, godparents or members of the parish team:
  Infant Baptism
  Confirmation
  First Communion
  Reconciliation

For adults as candidates, sponsors, godparents or members of the parish team:
  The Rite of Christian Initiation of Adults
  Marriage

Additional opportunities for parents

  Mothers' and toddlers' groups
  'Coffee and chat' groups – the year children start school
  Parenting programmes – the year either preceding or following the celebration of First Sacraments
  Another look at Reconciliation – when children are in Year 5
  Moving on – from primary to secondary school
  Teen-parenting programme – for parents of teenagers

Ministry training

In particular,
  Special ministers of the Eucharist
  Readers
  Liturgy teams
  Catechists
  Parish pastoral councils
  Bereavement visitors

'Life crisis' moments

In particular,
  Bereavement
  Divorce, marriage break-up
  Redundancy, unemployment, early retirement

Ongoing adult groups

(Based on the liturgical year)
  Bible study
  Senior citizens' faith-sharing/prayer groups
  'Reflections on the faith', e.g. short 5 or 6 week course or monthly sessions on aspects of Church teachings
  Parishioners with disabilities

Family life
Local community issues

If the sessions are to be *catechetical*, the kinds of material and resources used will vary according to the participants:

- their stage along their faith journey
- their questions, hopes and expectations
- their level of literacy
- their previous catechetical experience
- the time they can give.

You might find it helpful to read:
Adult Catechesis in the Christian Community, International Council for Catechesis, St Pauls Publishing, 1990.

4. Parents' Sessions in Context

In preparing to celebrate sacraments, there are some recognisable elements in a parish programme:

Candidates' preparation
- with their family
- with their teacher
- with their catechist
- with their parish community

Parents' preparation
- providing information about the candidates' preparation with an invitation and suggestions of how to support this at home
- looking at aspects of parenting, e.g. how to pray with children
- adult catechesis – accompanying adults on *their* faith journey

Liturgy
- celebrating stages along the journey of preparation.

Parish community involvement
- providing welcome, nurture, support, witness, prayer for the candidates and their families.

Pastoral visiting
- meeting families in their homes – reaching out, befriending, inviting, supporting, healing.

Team meetings
- offering initial and ongoing formation, leading to working in unison, better communication, as well as personal growth and faith development.

In planning Parents' Sessions it is essential to consider the following:
- how the proposed meetings fit into/relate to the total preparation: candidates' preparation, liturgical celebrations, parish community involvement, family visiting, team meetings
- the involvement of families not attending the parish school
- the involvement of families with children with learning disabilities
- the parent's sessions themselves, the place and timing of meetings, the content of meetings, the choice of themes, the team involved.

Family Links (see page 15) can be a useful source of contact with families.

> You might find it helpful to read *Sharing the Gift*, Paddy Rylands, Collins Liturgical Publications, 1989.

5. Family Links

Purpose

- to be a personal and direct link between the family and the parish community
- to be a support
- to be able to follow through any queries or problems as they emerge on a personal family level
- to help with communication
- to liaise with the parish priest and programme co-ordinator as appropriate.

NB: The link person is not intended to be a pastoral counsellor, solver of problems or go-between, but rather to enable the family to have an appropriate relationship with the parish so that the best preparation for first sacraments can take place.

Organisation

- each Family Link to link with a cluster of 4 to 5 families, preferably living in their neighbourhood.

Contact with families

- to deliver an invitation to enrol for the programme, and be able to explain the proposed preparation, responding to any queries
- to deliver an invitation to the first Parents' Session
- to welcome parents to the first session
- to introduce them to others in the 'cluster' group
- to take responsibility for gathering specific information, e.g. details of baptism, names for the certificate, etc., as requested by the programme co-ordinator
- to inform and invite families to participate in specific 'family' events in the parish
- to maintain contact, visiting as appropriate during the course of the year.

Who are the links?

- willing parishioners
- parents who have experienced the programme
- catechists
- parish sisters
- priests
- volunteers who have time, an ability to listen, are warm, friendly, non-judgemental, able to keep confidences, and have the good of these families at heart.

Formation for Family Links

- a clarification of the purpose, role and task
- basic listening skills
- an introduction to visiting skills
- an understanding of the overall preparation for First Sacraments

Planning and Preparation _____

1. Initial Planning

A framework for schools and parishes to use when planning their programme.

How are families invited to participate?

- letter from the parish priest?
- letter from the parish catechist?
- letter from school?
- visit from the parish priest?
- visit from the parish catechist?
- contact with the class teacher?
- parish newsletter?

What commitment is expected from parents?

- supporting their child's catechesis?
- bringing their child to Mass?
- full participation in the programme?

How is this to be formalised?

- enrolment Mass?
- enrolment form?
- interview with parish priest?

Who will lead the children's formal catechesis?

- school (in addition to the HIA[1] programme)?
- parish (in addition to the school HIA programme)? e.g. weekly/monthly sessions?
- family (in addition to the school HIA programme)?
- parish (in addition to the basic programme, WWM[2])?

Working with parents
   a. With what aim:

- explaining the child's preparation?
- involving the parents in the child's preparation?
- helping parents as parents?
- deepening understanding and faith?

1. HIA *Here I Am*, Ann Byrne, Chris Malone *et al*, HarperCollins, 1992

2. WWM *Walk With Me*, Anne White, McCrimmons Publishing Co. Ltd, 1996

b. Led by:
- school staff?
- parish priest?
- parish team?

c. Where:
- school?
- parish centre?
- church?
- home?

d. When:
- evenings?
- daytime?

Involvement in community liturgical celebrations
- in school?
- at parish Sunday Mass?
- with parish other than Sunday Mass?

Involvement of parish community
- in liturgical celebrations?
- as prayer sponsors/friends?
- as catechists?

Celebration of First Reconciliation
- as one large group?
- smaller groupings?
- families individually?
- Rite 1?
- Rite 2?

2. Planning the Timetable

Decide when the sacrament is to be celebrated and then plan your timetable. This proposal outline is intended to be adapted.

Approaches to the first celebration of the Sacrament of Reconciliation vary. The approach anticipated in the resources offered in this book is that it would be a communal penitential service with individual confession and absolution (Rite 2). It is recognised that parents will benefit from further catechesis when their children are preparing to celebrate Rite 1 (Year 5).

July or September	Session 1 (Introduction)
September	Session 2
October	Session 3
November	Session 4
Early Advent	Celebration of the Sacrament of Reconciliation

Some variations

a. The parents' sessions are offered on a weekly basis *prior* to the commencement of the children's preparation, with a 'practicalities' session shortly before the celebration of the sacrament.

Advantages

Parents get to know one another more quickly, names are remembered, trust and friendships build up and the discussion is subsequently entered into more deeply. Parents have an overview of the sacrament before the children's preparation begins.

Disadvantages

It may be hard to maintain contact with parents if they don't meet on a monthly basis. However, Family Links may overcome this disadvantage.

b. The first and last sessions are held as one large gathering, the 'middle' sessions are held in smaller, neighbourhood groups.

Advantages

Where there are large numbers involved, or where people are travelling from distances, this may lead to more personal communications.

Disadvantages

The sense of parish identity being developed through the whole group meeting together doesn't happen as quickly when the whole group is not meeting regularly – with careful organisation this is not insurmountable!

c. Offering a choice of times that parents can come to a session, e.g. evening or the following morning – perhaps making provision at the morning session for the presence of toddlers.

Advantages

It helps parents to realise you understand the realities of life!

Disadvantages

More time and effort is required from the team. With planning, this is not insurmountable.

3. Themes

It is intended that the themes are adapted according to the particular group of parents. Parishes may prefer to select their own titles. In general it brings a greater coherence to the programme if these correlate with the themes of the children's sessions and the celebrations.

Sacrament of Reconciliation

Session 1.   'Come and see'
             Introduction and Enrolment

Session 2.   'You are precious in my eyes'
             God – Calling Us into Relationship

Session 3.   'I did not come to call the virtuous, but sinners'
             Sin – Weakening/Breaking Our Relationship

Session 4.   'He was lost and is found'
             Reconciliation – Renewing Our Relationship

4. Including Parishioners with Disabilities

Integration means placing the individual within the desired group/community.

Inclusion entails being enabled to enter into relationship and gradually acquire an accepted and valued role so that there is a sense of mutuality within the group/community.

Why include parishioners with disabilities? This is what the Gospel calls us to do.

Paul reminds us that those who seem to be the weakest are the indispensable ones (1 Corinthians 12:22).

If we exclude people with disabilities, we lose a great richness and diversity and are the poorer. We deprive the whole Christian community of part of its natural growth in building up the Body of Christ.

We are a pro-life Church and must show this by our commitment to welcome into our community people with disabilities, from the developing foetus to the child, the adult and the elderly person, with all that person's experiences and gifts.

> Respect for the human person considers the other 'another self'. It presupposes respect for the fundamental rights that flow from the intrinsic dignity of the person.
>
> *Catechism of the Catholic Church*, para. 1944
> Geoffrey Chapman, 1995

In welcoming people we enter into relationship with them. Learning to relate and to communicate with each other is an essential part of living, of loving and of entering into a relationship with God.

Parents, whether or not their children attend special schools, rightly hope they will be seen as part of the Christian community. Finding ways of accomplishing this often requires extra thought and planning. Welcoming and *including* disabled children and adults does not always mean full participation in the parish programmes for catechetics – sometimes it does. There are many ways of positively including people and celebrating together. Our responsibility is to find those ways and ensure that reception of a particular sacrament marks a deepening of inclusion in the Church and parish.

© Rosemary McCloskey and June Edwards
St Joseph's Pastoral Centre, Diocese of Westminster

Essential reading
Valuing Difference: People with Disabilities in the Life and Mission of the Church, The Bishops' Conference of England and Wales, Department for Catholic Education and Formation, 1998.

You might find it helpful to read:

General Directory for Catechesis, paragraphs 37, 42, 133, Catholic Truth Society, 1997.

Sharing Our Faith – Involving People With Learning and Communication Difficulties in the Spiritual Life of the Parish, June Edwards, Matthew James Publishing Ltd, 1997.

Sharing Our Faith – Celebrating First Eucharist, June Edwards, Matthew James Publishing Ltd, 1997.

Sharing Our Faith – Celebrating Confirmation, June Edwards, Matthew James Publishing Ltd, 1997.

Developmental Disabilities and Sacramental Access, ed. Edward Foley. In particular, Chapter 5, 'Canonical Rights to The Sacraments', John Huels. The Liturgical Press, Minnesota, 1994.

5. Journeying with parents – preparing a foundation

Preparing to celebrate Reconciliation can be a very important time for parents in renewing and deepening their own faith.

To prepare for this some schools/parishes invite parents to come together for a series of gatherings in the first or second year of their child's schooling

- to develop friendships
- to build up community
- to give experience of working in groups
- to give the opportunity to share questions that are of concern.

Such an experience reduces the shyness and awkwardness that can dominate the early sessions of the preparation for first sacraments.

Useful resources
Noughts to Sixes Parenting Programme, M. and T. Quinn, Family Caring Trust, 1995 (for meetings with parents of young children).

Moments that Matter. Book 1: Starting School, Pastoral Formation Department, Archdiocese of Liverpool, Rejoice Publications, 1995.

'Coffee and chat' groups hosted by a catechist/parishioner with an informal agenda arising from topics parents want to discuss.

Helpful Hints for the Catechist _____

1. The Team

Gathering the team

The 'team' involves all those taking responsibility for a different part of the meeting. It could include any/all of the following. Adapt the team according to your resources.

- Priest: is he pastor? spiritual guide? visitor to each family? catechist? resource? The priest's role on the team requires clarification.
- Programme co-ordinator: to co-ordinate the overall programme, ensuring the appropriate partnership of home, school and parish, as well as the various team members.
- Catechist: to work with the parents, leading into and developing the theme.
- Candidates' teacher/catechist: to explain to parents what the preparation of the children involves and how the parents can support this at home.
- Parent: to share ways of living the theme in the family setting.
- Liturgy Link: explaining what is happening in the proposed liturgy and inviting the parents' participation.
- Family Link: welcoming the parents, helping with refreshments.

Once the team is gathered

Discuss together

- What formation and preparation have our team had?
- What ongoing support do members need/want?

Weak and Wobbly Hearts

Christian action is done by you and me, ordinary people with weak and wobbly hearts who do not have the security of trained skills, etc. I think Christian action and the promotion of the Kingdom is done by those who are afraid of what people will say, who are a bit cowardly, who are a bit diffident about standing up in public, do not have the security of plenty of practice and experience, can be capsized by failure, hurt by remarks, hurt by being ignored; find themselves reacting jealously when they do not want to, are overcome by despair, yet go on loving and trusting. It is the weak and wobbly hearts that Christ chooses, as he chose Peter, James, John, Thomas – all the disciples. They were not the high fliers of Galilee or Judaea, they were the ordinary folk, capable of love.

Letting Go in Love, Fr John Dalrymple
Darton, Longman & Todd, 1986

Pause for thought
*Have **you** ever felt like this?*

Questions for the team

Questions for the team to consider when meeting to plan the programme, focusing on *this* group of parents:

1. What are our hopes/concerns as we begin this programme?

2. How as a team do we work? Who does what? What time? How often will we meet? Where?

3. Who is the leader? Who do parents see as the leader? What's the role of the parish priest, headteacher, catechist – each member of the team?

4. Why are the parents gathering?

5. What are their expectations?

6. What commitment are we expecting from participants? How will this be agreed?

7. What timing, balance, plan of the session is most appropriate for this group?

8. How do we build relationships with the group members?

9. Are there different personalities: angry? shy? hurt? How do we respond to them?

10. Are there undercurrents? hidden agenda?

11. What is the previous experience history of the group? For example, have they been involved in a parenting programme? other sacramental programmes?

12. What is the starting point for this group? For example, white dresses(!), divorce/remarriage? What are the questions *this group of parents* want to discuss? How will the team respond?

13. Are there other questions/issues team members want to raise?

You might find it helpful to read:

The Sign We Give, Bishops' Conference of England & Wales, Matthew James Publishing Ltd, 1995.

Journeying together in faith

Catechesis is about accompanying others on their faith journey as they seek to deepen their relationship with Christ. You have the privilege of walking with others for a few months of their life-long journey.

The starting point is the present stage of others: start from where they are.

Be sensitive to the feelings of the parents – for many this may be their first experience of adult catechesis and of working in groups.

If this is the first contact of some parents with the Church since their child's baptism, some of their questions/comments may be:

- I can't go to Communion.
  I've been married twice.
  What's the point of coming to Mass?
- I've not been married in Church.
- I'm divorced.
  I feel I've no place in the Church.
- I'm not a Catholic, what's it all about?
- I've not been to Church for years.
  It's all changed; it doesn't make sense any more.

In your team's preparation, discuss together, particularly with the parish priest, how you will respond to these pastoral needs if they surface.

If, at the introductory meeting, a series of questions emerge, and you feel it is appropriate to base the subsequent sessions on these, do so! Hopefully the resources provided will help you to plan such sessions.

Catechesis is about sharing faith. Be ready to *listen* as well as to talk.

Remember – you too are invited to journey!

You might find it helpful to read:
Our Faith Story, A. P. Purnell, Collins, 1985.

Standing in another's shoes – an initial reflection for team members

Catechesis invites us to journey in faith with another. Sometimes it can be helpful when we start with a new group to pause, step out of our own shoes and attempt to stand in the shoes of those with whom we hope to journey, to glimpse life from their perspective. Take time to do the following exercise.

Think of a parent you know who wants his/her child to celebrate the Sacrament of Reconciliation.

Stand in that person's shoes. Spend a few moments reflecting on the realities of their life.

Using the word 'I', describe, for instance, their family, domestic, social, financial or spiritual situation.

In that person's shoes, try to explore:
- What bothers me most?
- What gives me life?
- What do I hope for?
- What destroys or takes away my life?
- What do I see when I look at the Church?
- What might the Church have to offer me?
- What am I expecting from the Church for my child as we prepare to celebrate this sacrament?

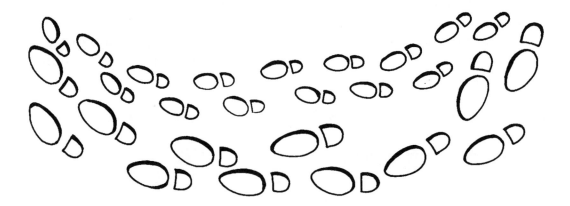

As you step back into your own shoes, what insights have you gained from this reflection? Take time to write these down. Share them with the team. As you listen to one another, be aware of how your reflections might affect your planning.

(Adapted with permission from an exercise used by Pat Jones)

2. The Session in Outline

Framework of a session

Apart from the introductory session, for which a particular framework is suggested, the material for each session is divided into the following sections:

1. Preparing the session
2. Welcome and introduction
3. Leading into the theme: describe and explore
4. Developing the theme: listen
5. Reflecting on the theme: reflect and relate to life
6. Living the theme
7. Celebrating the theme
8. Praying the theme
9. Closing the meeting.

Length of session: 1 hour 30 minutes.

NB: Don't forget to plan when you are going to have refreshments.

The content offered is primarily adult catechesis, drawing considerably on the scriptures. In the structure suggested, time is allocated towards the end of each session for the group to reflect on how, as parents, in the light of all that has been shared, they will be able to help their children to grow in faith. You may prefer to reverse the order by beginning the session with the practical issues relating to parents/parenting and then focus on the catechetical dimension.

At some stage during the course of the sessions it will obviously be necessary to deal with all the practicalities concerning the celebration of Reconciliation – the time for this will vary according to the local situation. Decide when and where it fits in with *your* sessions and plan accordingly.

For each session for Reconciliation, suggestions for a 'Family Sheet' are given. It is anticipated that this will be taken home. Please adapt it! (See, for example, the two pages following on page 53.)

Page 1. Introducing the theme
Page 2. Developing the theme
Page 3. Suggestions for living and celebrating the theme at home, at Mass.
(Space is allocated for notes concerning what the children are asked to complete in their workbooks this month.)
Page 4. Suggestions for prayer
(Space is allocated for writing in dates for the diary.)

The family sheet alone could be used with parents as a discussion starter where preparation is taking place more informally.

The sections of the session

The Pastoral Cycle – a way of working

Leading into the theme	DESCRIBE AND EXPLORE
Developing the theme	LISTEN
Reflecting on the theme	REFLECT AND RELATE TO LIFE
Celebrating the theme	PRAY AND CELEBRATE

This is based on a process, a methodology generally known as the 'Pastoral Cycle'.

For some, it is recognised in the more familiar form of SEE, JUDGE, ACT. This is a model created by the Belgian priest Joseph Cardign and used in his work with Young Christian Workers in the period between the two world wars. It remains in use in YCW and YCS work today.

The Pastoral Cycle was developed from this model by liberation theologians. We see it strongly reflected in the work of Paulo Freire and Juan Luis Segundo. It is a methodology for LIFE.

- It invites those involved to stand back and see what is happening, to NAME/ DESCRIBE and then to EXPLORE it – asking the who/what/why questions. A clearer picture of why things are as they are can emerge at this stage.
- The next stage is to LISTEN to appropriate scripture, the Church's tradition, teachings, doctrine, history, experience – so broadening the vision.
- This listening is followed by REFLECTION leading to APPROPRIATION – that is, making it part of *my* life.
- Through this reflective process, change becomes possible, resulting in ACTION.
- This shared experience is a cause for CELEBRATION.

In more recent years, the Pastoral Cycle has become the accepted process for Religious Education and catechesis. It reflects catechetical principles.

A more detailed study of the Pastoral Cycle illustrates that it reflects the movement in the Emmaus story (Luke 24) of the disciples coming to a deeper faith in the Lord, and, in fact, models the way the Lord journeys with the two disciples.

In working with adults, it is a recommended approach because

- it recognises, respects and takes seriously their life experience
- it recognises the importance of the Church's tradition – scripture, teachings, doctrine – informing that experience
- it invites change, action, growth, development and conversion, essential for Christian discipleship and mission in the world today.

You might find it helpful to read:

Christian Religious Education, Thomas Groome. Harper and Row, 1980

Let's Do Theology, Laurie Green. Mowbray, 1990.

Structure of the session

Welcome and introduction

Many parents have rushed to arrive in time for the session. They come from having sorted out meals, children, bedtime, baby-sitters – all that goes on in a household in the early evenings. Their minds may well still be with all that was going on in the house before they left, wondering if the children are all right, what *did* happen in that last ten minutes of *Coronation Street,* etc. etc! To 're-orientate' themselves suddenly into the preparation for Reconciliation may take a few minutes. Much will have happened in the lives of people since the last session, so a sensitive introduction can help people settle into the session more quickly. For example, if there has been a parish liturgy for the group since the last session, reference to it at this point can help to focus thoughts; or comment could be invited on how they managed with the suggestions for 'living the theme'. Drawing attention to the 'focal point' can be a way of opening up this session's theme.

Consider what opening prayer is appropriate.

Team member   Programme co-ordinator
Time allocation   5 minutes

Leading into the theme: describe and explore

The purpose of this part of the session is to enable participants to get in touch with their own experience of the particular theme, their 'story'. Various suggestions/ worksheets are given as ways of leading into each theme. It is for the catechist to select what would be most appropriate for their group, and to introduce it as a spoken/written task.

Rather than organise small group discussion (which involves moving chairs and disturbing people just as they have settled) the suggestion at this point is that once people have had the chance for quiet reflection, they are then invited to 'buzz' (share thoughts) with those on either side. An opportunity for group discussion will be given later.

The feedback can be recorded on the flipchart and provide the lead into the next part of the session.

- An alternative to the flipchart: pieces of wallpaper attached to the wall, pattern side against the wall.

- It is useful to keep a supply of pens and 'rest boards' for using with worksheets. ('rest boards'– pieces of thick card slightly bigger than the worksheets made from cardboard boxes and covered with wallpaper.)

Team member   Catechist
Time allocation   5-10 minutes, depending on the task.

Developing the theme: listen

During this part of the session time is given for 'input', for sharing scripture, the Church's story, teaching and traditions. For many adults this is their first experience of such an opportunity since leaving school. A variety of ways of presentation can be used – talks, video, fact sheet, slides with text, film strip, passages from the Bible or other suitable texts to name but some. Diocesan RE centres provide useful resources. New material is constantly being published – it is as well for the catechist to be alerted to this. In the notes provided, resources are suggested, *please adapt!* Particular references from the scriptures are given. For many adults, to present the theme from this scriptural dimension is to open up a whole new world – yet one that is vital for those striving to live a Christian, Gospel-centred life.

It is anticipated that the catechist, having decided on which aspect of the theme they are going to take, will prepare a presentation from the resources available according to the needs of the group.

Team member   Catechist
Time allocation   10 minutes

Reflecting on the theme: reflect and relate to life

Suggested questions based on the theme are offered – adapt them accordingly. The feedback from each group will allow the opportunity for further input if necessary, as well as allowing individuals to begin to relate all that they have heard to their *own* lives. Points to develop at the next session may emerge from this discussion. Be alert!

Team member   Catechist
Time allocation   Group work, 15 minutes
                          General feedback, 15-20 minutes

Living the theme

a. The family at home:

Suggestions are given on each 'Family Sheet' for ways for parents to develop the theme at home. In addition there may be requests from the candidate's teacher/catechist for parents to follow through particular work. This is a useful time to share these with the parents and to offer them encouragement.

b. The family at Mass:

Suggestions are given on the 'Family Sheet' to enable parents to help to focus their child's attention at Mass, gradually leading to greater participation in the Eucharist.

Team member   Teacher/Catechist/Parent
Time allocation   10 minutes

Celebrating the theme

Some parishes integrate regular liturgies into their programme of preparation. It is helpful if parents are given the necessary details, especially if they are going to be invited to be involved in a particular way. Parents who are unfamiliar with the Mass can find the liturgies somewhat bemusing and consequently find it hard to participate.

Suggestions for an Enrolment Service for Reconciliation are given on page 64.

Team member   Priest/catechist/Liturgy Link
Time allocation   5 minutes

Praying the theme

Resources are provided for a short period of prayer/meditation to draw the session to a close. In this busy, noisy and cluttered life, many parents really appreciate the opportunity for silence and prayer that such meditation can offer. To make use of the variety of ways of praying suggested in the resources means the catechist may be leading individuals to discover new ways of praying: the heart of catechesis, of which the aim is to put people 'not only in touch but in communion, in intimacy with Jesus Christ' (*Catechesi Tradendae*, para. 5).

Team member   Programme co-ordinator/catechist/priest
Time allocation   5-7 minutes

Closing the meeting

Allow time for any final comments, such as queries, notices to be given, etc. Try to ensure parents are not going home confused and upset. Thank the parents for coming. Make sure the team is available if individual parents need to chat.

Team member   Programme co-ordinator

After the meeting

The team

- tidies the room
- shares initial comments about the meeting
- decides/confirms who will follow-through with any parents missing from the meeting
- checks each member has the details of the date, time and venue for the next meeting

3. Preparation

Practical preparation – setting the scene

Room preparation

- What is the layout of the room?
- How are the chairs arranged – do they suggest sharing/discussion (semi-circle) or instruction (straight lines facing the speaker's desk)?
- Is the team separated from the parents by the barrier of a big desk, or are they a part of the circle?
- What focal point suggests the theme of the session?
- What in the arrangement, decoration and atmosphere of the room is going to encourage parents to enjoy and participate in the session?
- Are the necessary facilities easily available and clearly marked?
- Are the heating and lighting adequate?
- Can the flipchart be seen?

Welcome and hospitality

- Who greets the parents?
- Are name badges worn?
- How is a record of attendance kept? (It can be helpful to write the name of each child or family on their Family Sheet and place these on a table for the parents to collect as they arrive. Those left at the end of the evening indicate the absentees.)
- When are refreshments to be given? Served by whom?

Leadership

- Is it sensitive? listening? informed? respectful? competent?

Session

- Are the required materials at hand?
- How visual are the visual aids?
- How audible are audio aids?
- How well presented are the handouts? Do they respect the literacy level of the group? meet the needs of any illiterate adults?
- Is it planned to involve everyone? How?

In the notes for each session a 'Planning Sheet' is offered to help with the preparation.

Reminders for a first session

- What welcome and hospitality is there?

- What does the arrangement of the room say to people?

- What are people feeling, coming for the first time?

- Do we put people off by asking them to do things before they are ready to do so?

- Do we make people feel inadequate by the way we speak, do things?

- Do we frighten people by giving them pens, papers as soon as they walk through the door?

- Are we aware of the previous experiences of group members?

- Do people know what is happening: tonight? in the following sessions?

- What fun and enjoyment is there?

- What are we going to do that sends people home feeling affirmed and valued? (And making them look forward to coming back!)

- What would *you* add to this list?

In working with people, do not try to call them back to where they were, and do not try to call them to where you are, as beautiful as that place might seem to you. You must have the courage to go with them to a place that neither you nor they have been before.

Christianity Rediscovered, Vincent Donovan
SCM Press, 1978

Presenting the theme – an overview

Leading into the theme

Plan how you will encourage the participants to name and reflect on their experience of the theme/topic.

Developing the theme

Prepare 'input' from the richness of the scriptures, the Church's tradition and teachings. (Appropriate presentation, with variation over a number of sessions, is vital.)

Reflecting on the theme

Offer suitable questions/topics for discussion and sharing, arising from the 'input' for small groups.

Allow time for feedback from the whole group.

Living the theme

Relate the theme to everyday living, especially family life.

Share together ways in which it can be
a. lived at home
b. linked in with the celebration of the Eucharist.

Celebrating the theme

Explain what liturgy is planned for the group, and how each family is invited to participate.

Praying the theme

Choose an appropriate way of praying with which to end the session.

NB: When will refreshments be served?

Planning a focal point

Focal points, well prepared, can speak to the parts of us that words fail to reach.

As you plan your session, discuss together what visual presentation of the theme you can offer, using pictures? objects? fabrics? colour? icons? candles? incense?

Is it a different focal point each session, or one built up over the series of sessions, reflecting their progression?
Be simple!
Be creative!
Be thoughtful!
Be bold!

Presenting the theme – preparing yourself

Spend time reflecting on the theme.
- Let it buzz around *your* head for some days before the meeting.
- Begin to get in touch with how it relates to *your* experience.
- How is it part of *your* life?

Use the theme as a basis for your prayer.

Recall to mind your group.
- It is these whom you are accompanying on their faith journey.

Summarise in a sentence the content of the theme you hope to present.

From your experience:
- What are the most successful ways of stimulating the parents' participation and involvement?

- What kind of material and presentation is most appropriate for them?

Using the resources provided:
- Plan how you will 'set the scene' (see page 32).

- Plan how to lead into the theme.
  Select from the material offered.
  Interest is maintained if you can vary the approach from meeting to meeting.

- Prepare your 'input'.
  What story from everyday life are you going to use to introduce it?
  Reflect on the resources offered.
  What appropriate passages from scripture could you use?
  What particular parts from the Church's tradition are you going to share?

Prepare the questions to stimulate reflection and discussion.
- Are those offered in the resources suitable for your group?

Choose a closing meditation/prayer to reflect the theme.
- Are the resources offered appropriate?

After the meeting, with the whole team if possible, reflect on all that happened:
- What do we need to carry through to the next session?
- What would you change in your approach next time?

It is valuable for the whole team to discuss these points.

4. The Session in Practice

Leading a session

- Make sure the meeting room is warm, well lighted and comfortable.

- Welcome each person.

- Use people's names when speaking with them.

- Clarify the purpose of the session. Confirm this is agreed and accepted by all.

- Agree the 'boundaries', e.g. all that is spoken remains confidential, only one person speaks at a time so that all can hear . . .

- Affirm each contribution made.

- Invite participation of *all* members.

- Be alert for the less confident, less articulate members.

- Foster acceptance of individual opinions/feelings.

- Use your gift of humour!

- Befriend silence.

- Ensure the set task is achieved – as far as possible.

- Finally, thank the group for their participation.

Working with groups

Begin by
- inviting people to introduce themselves. This helps to build friendship in the group, it can be easier to talk with friends rather than strangers.

Explain
- All that is shared in groups is confidential.
- There are no 'First Prizes'! It is parents' thoughts and comments that are being invited, rather than knowledge being tested.
- The invitation is to *listen* rather than argue or debate.
- When worksheets are filled in, these are for the individual's eyes only. (No one else will be looking at them: it does not matter how good or bad a person's spelling or drawing may be, no one else will see the worksheet.)

Finally
- Ask the group to appoint a spokesperson to give any feedback.

Feedback
- Take the feedback from each group in turn before starting any general discussion.
- Record it on the flipchart. This helps the group to 'own' it.
- Once all the feedback is recorded:
  - glance over it
  - decide which points you will leave until next time – with the agreement of the group
  - decide which points you will deal with immediately – and do so.
- Try to draw things together on a positive note.

Remember
- Be sensitive! What *you* have offered in the 'input' may be new to some parents.
- A helpful way of stimulating group participation is to invite:
  - individual reflection
  - then sharing in two's
  - followed by sharing in the small group.

You might find it helpful to read:
Working with Groups, CAFOD, 1986.

Using scripture

> *The Word of God is something alive and active: it cuts like any double-edged sword but more finely* (Hebrews 4:12).

- The way we pick up, hold, reverence the Bible, all speak of the importance we give the Word.

- The Hebrew scriptures are part of our shared tradition with the Jewish people and so should be treated with respect for their tradition as well.

- If appropriate, set the passage in context. Scripture is the Word of God and that Word is spoken to us today. However, it was written at a particular historical period and some awareness of the background can help us to deepen and enrich our interpretation and understanding of God's Word.

- Invite listeners to prepare themselves to hear the Word before it is proclaimed.

- Allow the Word to convey its own message to the listener.

- Invite listeners to share what they have heard, so enriching one another.

- Follow the listening and shared reflection with a pause for quiet prayer, allowing individuals time to make their own response to the Word spoken.

You might find it helpful to read:
Focus on the Bible, H. J. Richards, Kevin Mayhew Ltd, 1989.
Not Counting Women and Children, Megan McKenna, Orbis Books, 1994.
Gospel Light, John Shea, The Crossword Publishing Co., 1998.

Praying the theme

- Over the series of sessions, vary the type of prayer experience offered. People pray in different ways. Some are particularly grateful for having new ways of prayer offered to them.

- Create an atmosphere for prayer,
  e.g. light a candle, play quiet music, turn down the lighting.

- Draw attention to the focal point,
  e.g. icon, Bible, candle, screen if slides are to be used.

- *Invite* the group to participate – not all will be in the mood for praying. Some may prefer to sit quietly. Respect this.

- Give a brief outline of what is involved.

- Lead into the prayer from the discussion using the theme of the session.

- Prayer content: opening hymn/prayer – reading – pause for individual, then shared, reflection – invitation to share intercessions.

- Draw the prayer to an end in a definite way – with a hymn or blessing, for example:
  May the Lord bless you and keep you.
  May the Lord let his face shine on you
     and be gracious to you.
  May the Lord uncover his face to you
     and bring you peace.
  (Numbers 6:24-26)

- At some stage during the prayer, invite all the group to participate vocally, e.g. 'For all we have shared this evening we praise and thank the Father, praying, "Glory be to the Father . . ."' (said by all) or singing a simply worded hymn, e.g. 'Be still and know that I am God'.

Be adventurous!

- Use quiet music as a background to readings.
- Use slides to illustrate readings.
- Use taped songs that are familiar to the group so they can join in the refrain. (These could be illustrated with one, or a series of slides.)
- Use readings involving a number of voices (allow readers to prepare).
- Use silence!

You might find it helpful to read:

Helping Children to Pray, R. Cardwell, The Grail, 1981.

Biblical Prayers, L. Deiss, World Library Publications, 1976.

Starting Points, Sr Judith Russi SSMN, Geoffrey Chapman, 1991.

The Edge of Glory, David Adam, Triangle/SPCK, 1985.

Praying with Children, Jenny Pate, McCrimmons, 1995.

Reviewing progress

1. Who has taken the *responsibility* for the sessions – school? parish? partnership of both?

2. Has the *main thrust* of the meetings been parenting? giving information? adult catechesis?

3. How were the *meetings organised* – one large group? small groups around the parish? individual families with a catechist?
   How appropriate was this?

4. How are families with children *with learning disabilities/special needs* included?

5. How are families with children *not attending the parish school* included?

6. What has been the involvement of the *parish community*?

7. What has been the place of *liturgy* during the preparation – parish Sunday Eucharist? parish non-Eucharist service? school assembly? school Mass?

8. How successful have the *Family Links* been in establishing and maintaining contact with families?

9. What contact/*pastoral visiting* has there been with families with minimal participation in the programme?

10. What *networking* has taken place to share/develop additional resources?

11. What *follow-up* to the programme is planned? How will it be organised? by whom? when?

12a. At what stage is specific preparation for Rite 1 (private confession with individual absolution) offered? What help and support is given to parents?

  b. If Rite 2 (general penitential service with individual absolution) is the form for First Confession, how is this developed? For example, is there a penance service for children at regular intervals – Advent, Lent, Pentecost? Is this in the parish or school?

13. Have *you* any other thoughts, queries, comments, suggestions . . .?

PART 2
Resources for Reconciliation

Introduction _____

This resource contains material for sessions with parents whose children are preparing to celebrate the Sacrament of Reconciliation. They are prepared for catechists offering a parish-based programme of preparation in partnership with the school and family. It is envisaged that catechists will be drawing on other resources for the children's preparation, for the community involvement, the liturgies during the preparation and the first celebration of the Sacrament of Reconciliation.

The material is offered in the form of four sessions:

Session 1. 'Come and see'
            Introduction and Enrolment

Session 2. 'You are precious in my eyes'
            God – Calling Us into Relationship

Session 3. 'I did not come to call the virtuous, but sinners'
            Sin – Weakening/Breaking Our Relationship

Session 4. 'He was lost and is found'
            Reconciliation – Renewing Our Relationship

Within each session, there are resources for inviting parents:
• to listen to suggestions for supporting the work of their child's teacher/catechist;
• to reflect on what they can do at home as their child's 'first teacher in the ways of faith';
• to deepen their own understanding of this sacrament;
• to reflect on their own faith journey;
• to pray together.

In addition there is:
• a passage for the catechists' personal reflection on the theme;
• a planning sheet to help the catechists with their practical preparation;
• a planning sheet for the closing prayer;
• a sample presentation the catechist might offer to parents;
• a Family Sheet for parents to take home.

Please *adapt* the material according to the requirements of your group of parents.

Initial Team Preparation

This material is only a tool – and any tool is only as good as its operator! Part 1, Guidelines for Catechists, provides a background for using these resources, as well as an explanation about their structure and organisation.

Before staring work with parents:
- Read through Part 1.
- Share any reflections.
- Work through any queries or difficulties.
- Ensure all team members are happy with the basic structure and organisation suggested in Part 1.
- Discuss any adaptations you may need to make.
- Decide the roles and responsibilities of individual team members.
- Agree the programme timetable – dates, times and venue.

As well as your skill as catechists, it is your team's understanding of Reconciliation that will influence how well you accompany parents. As you prepare yourselves, it is recommended that the team take time to reflect together on the following questions:
- What does Reconciliation mean for us?
- What do we want to share about the Sacrament of Reconciliation with this group of parents?

Essential background reading:

Reconciliation for the Millennium, The Bishops' Conference of England and Wales, Catholic Truth Society, 1999.

Programme timetable

Parents' sessions

VENUE _____

TIMES
Start _____ Finish _____

DATES
Session 1 _____ Session 3 _____

Session 2 _____ Session 4 _____

Team planning meetings

VENUE _____

TIMES
Start _____ Finish _____

DATES
Session 1 _____ Session 4 _____

Session 2 _____ Session 5 (Evaluation) _____

Session 3 _____

Celebrations

VENUE _____

TIMES
Start _____ Finish _____

DATES
Celebration 1 _____ Celebration 3 _____

Celebration 2 _____ Celebration 4 _____

Children's meetings (For information to help with the planning)

Dates _____

_____

Session 1. 'Come and see'

Introduction and Enrolment

General outline

It is recommended that the setting for this introductory meeting is informal, welcoming and friendly – consider beginning with refreshments (coffee/cake or cheese/wine?). Many of the parents coming may be unfamiliar with parish buildings/structures. It helps if, prior to the meeting, all parents have been visited by a member of the team (Family Link) who then welcomes them on arrival, introduces them to other parents and ensures they have refreshments. This will help to develop a sense of community in the group.

Preparing the session

Focal point
Symbols/pictures reflecting the theme of the session,
e.g. purple stole, candle, crucifix, Bible.

Welcome

Formally welcome the group. Thank the parents for coming. Introduce the team, explaining the role of each member. Invite the parents to introduce themselves to those sitting on either side. Explain the plan of the evening.

Listening and inviting

1. Invite parents to recall their own experience/memories/stories of First Confession. What kind of experience do they want it to be for their children? Allow time for discussion.

2. First Forgiveness/Reconciliation/Confession – what are we talking about? What name will be used in *this* parish preparation? Discuss this together, using page 55. Page 56 gives some background to the various names given to this sacrament.

3. Give an outline of the proposed programme in which parents are being invited to take part. This could be printed on the front page of the Family Sheet with relevant dates, times and venues. Explain what is proposed and *why* for each of the following areas:
   - The date of the celebration of the Sacrament of Reconciliation
   - How the children are being prepared in the school/parish, the role of the parents in this preparation
   - Provision for children attending schools other than the parish school
   - The place of the liturgies/celebrations
   - Prayer friend/prayer sponsors (i.e. parishioners willing to pray for one particular child each day as they prepare to celebrate the sacraments)

- Family Links (Guidelines, page 15)
- Parents' meetings. It is particularly important that the purpose of the parents' meeting is clarified. Many parents will be unfamiliar with the idea of such involvement with their child's preparation. It is unlikely that *their* parents would have come to meetings when they made their First Confession. It is not surprising if parents come with hesitation and questions.

Useful resources

Pope John Paul's words to First Communion parents at Cardiff (see page 58). Allow time for 'buzzing', questions, comments . . .

or

The Story by Brendan Kennelly (page 59). This could be followed by such questions as:

- Do we think our Christian Story should be retold?
- Does it make a difference to people's lives?
- What is the role of parents in children coming to know the story?
- How true is it that our faith affects our
      head (the way we think and understand)?
      heart (the way we relate, love . . .)?
      hands (the way we act)?

4. Introduce the three ways of celebrating this sacrament (page 60), pointing out the common elements. Explain which of the three rites the children will be using for their first celebration of the sacrament and why. Explain when they will be introduced to using the other rites. Explain the usual way adults celebrate this sacrament. Allow time for comment.

5. Look together at the 'Signs of Readiness' (page 61). Invite parents to reflect on which of the signs are already evident in their children. Discuss how they can expect their child to develop over the coming weeks. Explain how the children's formal teaching on this sacrament will continue in school through the remainder of the primary school years.

6. Introduce the 'Night Prayer' (Prayer for the end of the day; on the Family Sheet, following on page 53). Reviewing life is an integral part of the preparation for this sacrament. Encourage parents to consider using it regularly as a family prayer.

7. Invite parents to chat together to see if there are questions/issues to be raised. Allow time for feedback.

Invitation to enrol

Give out the enrolment forms (pages 62 and 63), inviting parents to complete and return them if they wish their family to take part in the programme.

Prayer

Using the resources, plan a closing prayer to reflect the theme of the session.

Closing the session
Thank the group for their participation.
Final words . . .

After the meeting
Tidying up and clarifying communication with families not represented at the meeting.

Team Preparation
Session 1: Planning sheet

1. Preparing yourselves

Share together your reflections on 'Pause and reflect . . .'
Reread 'Reminders for a first session', sharing any comments (Guidelines page 33).

2. Preparing for Session 1

Date _____ Time _____

Venue _____ Theme _____

3. Areas of responsibility   Team member

Publicity/reminder to parents
of the next meeting   _____

Setting the scene   _____

Focal point   _____

Refreshments   _____

Welcome and introduction   _____

Listening and inviting   _____

Invitation to enrol   _____

Closing the session   _____

After the session – tidying up   _____

Contacting absent parents   _____

Resources

Family Sheet: what adaptations?   _____

Worksheets/handouts to be duplicated   _____

Page numbers: _____ _____

❑ Flipchart   ❑ Felts   ❑ Tape recorder _____

Session 1: Planning prayer

Focal point _____

Creating a mood of prayer

lighting a candle yes/no

taped music   yes/no

taped song   yes/no

Invitation to pray

led by _____

Opening song/prayer

led by _____

Reading with/without music backing
        with/without slides

Pause for reflection with/without invitation to reread passage
              with/without invitation to pick out keywords/phrases

Invitation to share reflection

led by _____

Invitation to share intentions

led by _____

Closing words/song

led by _____

Session 1: Pause and reflect

As you read and reflect on this story, think back to your own childhood experience of the sacrament. What memories, thoughts, feelings are stirred? How might these parents be feeling?

MY FIRST CONFESSION

With the fear of damnation in my soul I went into the confessional and the door closed of itself behind me.

It was pitch dark and I couldn't see the priest or anything else. Then I really began to be frightened. In the darkness it was a matter between God and me, and he had all the odds. He knew what my intentions were before I ever started. I had no chance. All I had ever been told about confession got mixed up in my mind, and I knelt to one wall and said, 'Bless me Father, for I have sinned: this is my first confession'. I waited for a few minutes, but nothing happened, so I tried it on the other wall. Nothing happened there either. God had me spotted all right.

It must have been then that I noticed the shelf at about one height with my head. It was really a place for grown-up people to rest their elbows, but in my distracted state I thought it was probably the place where you were supposed to kneel. Of course, it was on the high side and not very deep, but I was always good at climbing and managed to get up all right. Staying up was the problem. There was room only for my knees, and nothing you could get a grip on but a sort of wooden moulding a bit above it. I held on to the moulding and repeated the words a little louder, and this time something happened all right. A slide was slammed back; a little light entered the box, and a man's voice said: 'Who's there?'

'Tis me, Father,' I said, for fear he mightn't see me and go away again. I couldn't see him at all. The place the voice came from was under the moulding, about level with my knees, so I took a good grip of the moulding and swung myself down till I saw the astonished face of a young priest looking up at me. He had to put his head on one side to see me, and I had to put mine on one side to see him. So we were more or less talking to one another upside down. It struck me as a queer way of hearing confessions, but I didn't feel it my place to criticise.

'Bless me, Father, for I have sinned; this is my first confession,' I rattled off, all in one breath, and swung myself down the least shade more to make it easier for him.

I lost my grip, tumbled and hit the door an unmerciful wallop. I found myself flat on my back in the middle of the aisle. The people who had been waiting stood up with their mouths open. The priest opened the door of the middle box and came out.

'Was it coming to confession you were, my poor man?' he asked me.

'Twas, Father,' I said with a sob.

'Oh, he said respectfully, 'a big hefty fellow like you must have terrible sins. Is this your first?'

'Tis, Father,' said I.

'Worse and worse,' he said gloomily. 'The crimes of a lifetime. I don't know, will I get rid of you all today. You'd better wait now till I'm finished with these old ones. You can see by the look of them they haven't much to tell.'

'I will, Father,' I said, with something approaching joy. It only stood to reason

51

that a fellow confessing after seven years would have more to tell than people that went every week. The crimes of a lifetime, exactly as he had said. It was only what he expected, and the rest was the cackle of old women and girls.

I started to make my examination of conscience, and barring the one bad business of wanting to kill my grandmother, it didn't seem so bad.

The next time, the priest steered me into the confession box himself and left the shutter back, the way I could see him get in and sit down at the further side of the grille from me.

'Well now' he said, 'What do they call you?'

'Jackie, Father' said I.

'And what's a-trouble to you, Jackie?'

'Father,' I said, feeling I might as well get it over while I had him in a good humour, 'I had it all arranged to kill my grandmother.'

He seemed quite shaken by that, all right, because he said nothing for quite a while.

'My goodness,' he said at last, 'that would be a shocking thing to do. What put that in your head?'

'Father,' I said, feeling very sorry for myself, 'she's an awful woman.'

'Is she?' he asked. 'What way is she awful?'

'She takes porter, Father,' I said, knowing well from the way Mother talked of it this was a mortal sin, and hoping it would make the priest take a more favourable view of my case.

'Oh, my!' he said, and I could see he was impressed.

'And snuff, Father,' said I.

'That's a bad case, sure enough, Jackie,' he said.

'And she goes round in her bare feet, Father,' I went on in a rush of self-pity, 'and she knows I don't like her and she gives pennies to my sister Nora and none to me, and my Da sides with her and flakes me, and one night I was so heart-scalded I made up my mind I'd have to kill her.'

'And what would you do with the body?' he asked, with great interest.

'I was thinking I could chop that up and carry it away in a barrow I have,' I said.

'Begor, Jackie,' he said, 'do you know you're a terrible child?'

'I know, Father,' I said, for I was just thinking the same myself. 'I tried to kill Nora, too, with a bread-knife, only I missed her.'

'You must have great courage,' he said. 'Between ourselves there's a lot of people I'd like to do the same to, but I'd never have the nerve. Hanging is an awful death.'

'Is it, Father?' I asked with the deepest interest – I was always very keen on hanging. 'Did you ever see a fellow hanged?'

'Dozens of them,' he said solemnly. 'And they all died roaring.'

'Jay!' I said.

'Oh, a horrible death!' he said, with great satisfaction. 'Lots of the fellows I saw killed their grandmothers too, but all said 'twas never worth it.'

He had me there for a full ten minutes talking, and then walked out the chapel yard with me.

Nora was sitting on the railing waiting for me, and she put on a very sour puss when she saw the priest with me. She was mad jealous because a priest had never come out of the church with her.

'Well,' she asked suspiciously after he had left me, 'what are you sucking?'

'Bullseyes.'

'Was it the priest gave them to you?'

'Twas,'

'Lord God,' she wailed bitterly, 'some people have all the luck! 'Tis no advantage to anybody trying to be good. I might as well be a sinner like you.'

Frank O'Connor, 'My First Confession', in
My Oedipus Complex and Other Stories
Penguin Books, 1963

Family Sheet and Session notes/handouts follow.

'Come and see'

Introduction and Enrolment

Celebrating Reconciliation

Our parish programme of preparation

Prayer for the end of the day

Think about all that has happened today, at home, at school, with your friends . . . .

Think about the happy things that have happened . . . .

Say 'Thank you' to God our Father for each of them.

Think about the times things have gone wrong today, the times you have caused unhappiness . . . .

Tell Jesus you are sorry.

Jesus,
I trust in your love and forgiveness.
I am sorry for all the wrong things I have done.
I am sorry for all the good things I have not done.
I want to love you with all my heart.
Amen.

Think about tomorrow . . . .

Ask the Holy Spirit to help you make it a happy day for all the people you meet.

Amen.

Things to remember

1. God *never* stops loving us.

2. Your child first learns about God's love and forgiveness from you.

3. In talking about the Sacrament of Reconciliation, the centre of the picture must always be God and God's love, not the negative aspect of sin.

4. Help your child to know God as a personal friend, who is interested in all s/he does. Encourage them to talk to God in their own words, and also to listen to God in moments of silence. The best way to teach your child to pray is to make prayer a real part of your own life.

5. At the end of each day, together thank God for giving each of you opportunities during that day to share God's love with those around you . . . mention specific moments, such as willingness to share toys etc.

6. Help your child to express sorrow if they have made anyone unhappy; again help them to think of particular incidents.

7. Don't dwell overmuch on your child's naughtiness. Don't keep reminding them of what they have done. Never say, 'You'll have to say that when you go to Confession!' Affirm the good!

Signs of readiness for the Sacrament of Reconciliation

Here are a few points to look out for. You won't see all of them all the time, but if you see some of them, some of the time, this is generally enough.

1. Does your child genuinely want to pray, at least now and again?

2. Does your child sometimes say 'sorry' without being made to?

3. Is your child able to forgive others when they say 'sorry' to him/her, or, occasionally when they don't say they're sorry?

4. Can your child accept some responsibility for his/her actions, or does s/he always blame someone else?

5. Does your child try to control his/her instincts (e.g. temper) at least now and again?

6. Does your child realise that a small thing done on purpose is more serious than a larger 'catastrophe' caused by accident?

If you feel that your child is not ready for this sacrament, don't force him/her. He or she may need time.

Adapted from 'Things to Remember' in *To God with Love and Sorrow* Brentwood Religious Education Service, St Pauls Publishing, 1975.

What happens when we go to confession?

- I meet with the priest to celebrate this sign of God's life in the world. He welcomes me and leads us in prayer.

- We listen to the word of God read from the Scriptures.

- I acknowledge past failures and past refusals to live as a Christian. I tell God I am sorry.

- The priest offers words of encouragement and a reminder of Christ's healing, welcoming love is given. A suggestion of an act of sorrow and reparation is made.

- I say an Act of Contrition.

- The priest extends his hand and says the Words of Absolution.

    God, the Father of mercies,
    through the death and resurrection of his Son
    has reconciled the world to himself
    and sent the Holy Spirit
    among us for the forgiveness of sins;
    through the ministry of the Church
    may God give you pardon and peace
    and I absolve you from your sins
    in the name of the Father,
    and of the Son, and of the Holy Spirit.

- I/we offer a final prayer of praise and thanksgiving to God.

Questions to think about

- Do you have childhood memories of Confession?

- Do you have memories of your own First Confession?

- With what understanding of the Sacrament of Forgiveness do you want your child to grow up?

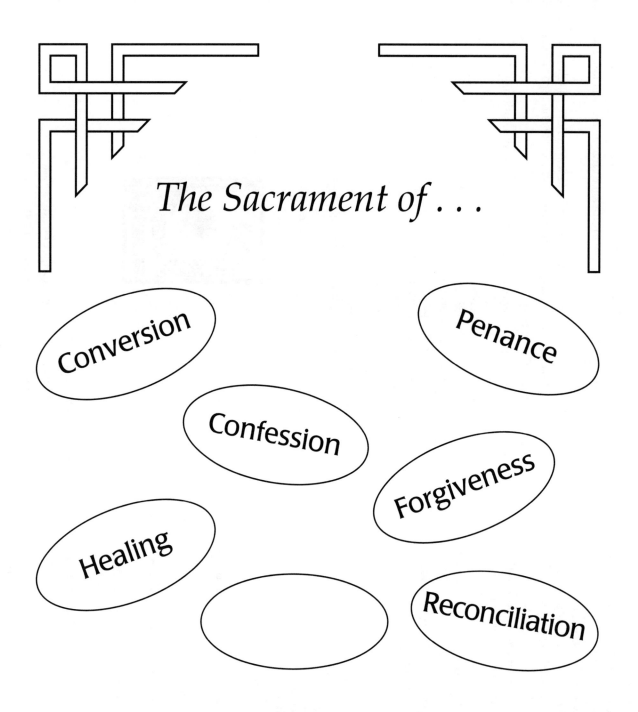

The Sacrament of . . .

Conversion

Penance

Confession

Forgiveness

Healing

Reconciliation

- Which word makes most sense to you as a name for the sacrament?

- Which of these words makes most sense for your child?

- What name would you like to use in the parish preparation?

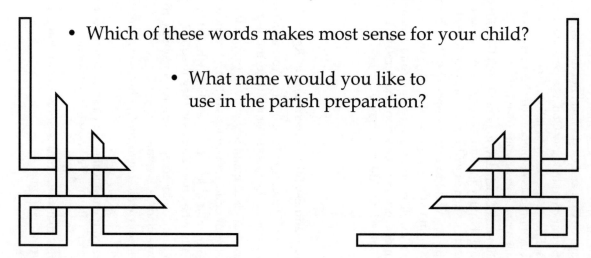

The Names We Give This Sacrament

It is called the *sacrament of conversion* because it makes sacramentally present Jesus' call to conversion, the first step in returning to the Father from whom one has strayed by sin.

It is called the *sacrament of penance*, since it consecrates the Christian sinner's personal and ecclesial steps of conversion, penance and satisfaction.

It is called the *sacrament of confession*, since the disclosure or confession of sins to a priest is an essential element of this sacrament. In a profound sense it is also a 'confession' – acknowledgement and praise – of the holiness of God and of his mercy towards sinful humankind.

It is called the *sacrament of forgiveness*, since by the priest's sacramental absolution God grants the penitent 'pardon and peace'.

It is called the *sacrament of reconciliation*, because it imparts to the sinner the love of God who reconciles: 'Be reconciled to God.' He who lives by God's merciful love is ready to respond to the Lord's call: 'Go; first be reconciled to your brother.'

Catechism of the Catholic Church, paragraphs 1423, 1424.
Geoffrey Chapman, 1994.

POPE JOHN PAUL II

Dear parents of these children: your love for Christ has made this day possible. For you are your children's teachers in the ways of faith. By what you say and do, you show them the truths of our faith and the values of the Gospel. This is indeed not only a sacred duty, but a grace, a great privilege. Many other members of the Church share in this task, but the main responsibility for your children's religious formation rests upon your shoulders. So try to make your homes genuinely Christian. Help your children to grow and mature as Jesus did at Nazareth, 'in wisdom, in stature and in favour with God and men'. Allow no one to take advantage of their lack of experience and knowledge. As you share with them in their personal pilgrimage to God, may you always be united in prayer and worship and in humble love of God and his people.

Address to parents of First Communion candidates, from
The Pope Teaches − The Pope in Britain
the complete texts, Catholic Truth Society, 1982

The Story

The story was not born with Robbie Cox
nor with his father
nor with his father's father
but farther back than any could remember.

Cox told the story
over twelve nights of Christmas.
It was the story
made Christmas real.
When it was done
the new year was in,
made authentic by the story.
The old year was dead,
buried by the story.
The man endured,
deepened by the story.

When Cox died,
the story died.
Nobody had time
to learn the story.
Christmas shrivelled,
the old year was dust,
the new year nothing special,
so much time to be endured.

The people withered.
This withering hardly troubled them.
The story was a dead crow in a wet field,
an abandoned house, a rag on a bush,
a sick whisper in a dying room,
the shaking gash of an old man's mouth
breaking like burnt paper
into black ashes the wind scatters,
people fleeing from famine.
Nobody has ever heard of them.
Nobody will ever speak for them.

I know the emptiness
spread by the story's death.
This emptiness is in the roads
and in the fields,
in men's eyes and children's voices,
in summer nights when stars
play like rabbits behind Cox's house,
house of the story
that once lived on lips
like starlings startled from a tree,
exploding in a sky of revelation,
deliberate and free.

Brendan Kennelly
from *A Time for Voices: Selected Poems 1960-1990*
Bloodaxe Books Ltd

The Different Forms for the Celebration of the Sacrament of Reconciliation

The *Ordo Paenitentiae*, 1974, provides three different rites for the celebration of the Sacrament of Reconciliation.

1. Reconciliation of individual penitents.
2. Reconciliation of a number of penitents with individual confession and absolution.
3. Reconciliation of penitents with communal confession and absolution.

Rite 1. Reconciliation of individual penitents

The setting for this is the confessional 'box' or room where priest and penitent can meet face to face.

- The priest greets and welcomes the penitent.
- A reading from the scriptures is optional.
- The penitent makes a confession of sins, with the help of the priest, expressing sorrow.
- The priest counsels the penitent, offering words of encouragement. He suggests a suitable penance – an act of sorrow and reparation and a help for amendment of life.
- The penitent says a prayer of sorrow.
- The priest says the words of absolution.
- A final prayer of thanksgiving.

Rite 2. Reconciliation of a number of penitents with individual confession and absolution

Often celebrated in Advent and Lent, this form of Reconciliation brings out the communal and ecclesial nature of sin. Services are generally based on the following framework:

- Opening hymn
- Greeting
  Introduction
  Opening prayer
- Celebration of God's Word
  Homily
- Examination of conscience
- General confession of sins (e.g. I confess . . .)
- Individual confession; expression of sorrow, suitable penance and absolution
- Hymn/prayer of praise
- Concluding prayer
- Blessing
- Final hymn

Rite 3. Reconciliation for penitents with communal confession and absolution

This rite is intended for use only in exceptional circumstances.

The form of the service is the same as for Rite 2 until after the homily.

- General confession – all those wishing to receive general absolution are invited to indicate their desire for it, e.g. kneel down. Then there is general confession, e.g. I confess . . . and imposition of penance.
- General absolution – the priest gives absolution with his hands stretched out over the penitents.
- Thanksgiving and concluding prayer.
- Final hymn.

Signs of Readiness

Does your child sometimes

* want to pray to God?

* say 'sorry' without being told?

* forgive others – even if they don't say 'sorry'?

* take responsibility for his/her actions, without blaming others?

* control instincts (e.g. temper)?

* know the difference between right and wrong?

* realise a small thing done on purpose is more serious than a larger 'disaster' caused by accident?

If you see some of these signs some of the time a child is generally ready to celebrate the sacrament.

Adapted from 'Things to Remember'
in *To God with Love and Sorrow*
Brentwood Religious Education Service
St Pauls Publishing, 1975

Parish of

_____

Preparing to Celebrate
The Sacrament of Reconciliation

CHILD'S NAME _____

ADDRESS _____

_____

TELEPHONE NUMBER _____

DATE OF BIRTH _____

PLACE AND DATE OF BAPTISM _____

I/We wish our child to be a part of the parish programme of Preparation for Reconciliation and will do our best to help and support

_____

SIGNED _____

DATE _____

FATHER'S NAME _____

RELIGION _____

MOTHER'S NAME _____

RELIGION _____

Please return this form to the Presbytery,
with a copy of the Baptism Certificate.

Parish of

_____

Preparing to Celebrate the Sacraments of Reconciliation and Holy Communion

CHILD'S NAME _____

ADDRESS _____

_____

TELEPHONE NUMBER _____

DATE OF BIRTH _____

PLACE AND DATE OF BAPTISM _____

I/We wish our child to be a part of the parish programme of Preparation for Reconciliation and Holy Communion and will do our best to help and support

_____

SIGNED _____

DATE _____

FATHER'S NAME _____

RELIGION _____

MOTHER'S NAME _____

RELIGION _____

Please return this form to the Presbytery,
with a copy of the Baptism Certificate.

Enrolment of candidates for First Sacraments

To be adapted
Renewal of baptismal promises (Replacing the Creed)
All stand

Priest	Parents, before you present your children to the parish to be prepared for First Forgiveness and Holy Communion, you are invited to witness to your faith, together with all here present, by renewing the promises of your baptism.
Priest	Do you believe in God, the Father Almighty, maker of heaven and earth?
All	We do.
Priest	Do you believe in Jesus Christ his only Son who became man for us?
All	We do.
Priest	Do you believe in the Holy Spirit who lives in our hearts?
All	We do.

The Priest addresses the families of the candidates, the rest of the congregation is invited to sit.

Priest	Dear parents, what is it you ask of God's Church for your child?
Parents	First Forgiveness and Holy Communion.
Priest	Are you willing to do your best to help your child to prepare to celebrate these sacraments?
Parents	We are, with the help of God.

The Priest blesses the medals, then invites the candidates and their families to come forward. Each child brings her/his name card and offers it to the Priest who exchanges it for a medal, after addressing the candidate in these or similar words:

Priest	N . . . , do you want to get ready to receive your First Forgiveness and Holy Communion?
Candidate	Yes, please!
Priest	N . . . , wear this medal as a sign of being in the preparation group in our parish.

Priest places medal around the neck of the candidate.

The congregation could be invited to sing an appropriate hymn during this time.

The Liturgy continues with the Prayer of the Faithful.

After Mass, the name cards could be displayed in an appropriate part of the church for the rest of the time of the programme, inviting the congregation to pray for the candidates.

NB: If there is a large group of children, catechists could be invited to help with the distribution of the medals.

Session 2. 'You are precious in my eyes'

God – Calling Us into Relationship

General outline

Preparing the session

Focal point

Symbols/pictures reflecting the theme of the session, e.g. icon of the Lord, Bible, baptismal candle, water/bowl.

Welcome

Welcome the group. Opening prayer. Invite the parents to introduce themselves to the person sitting on either side. Introduce the team. Explain the plan of tonight's meeting and how it fits into the overall programme. Allow time for comments from parents.

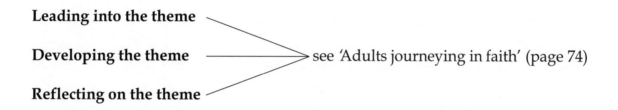

Leading into the theme

Developing the theme — see 'Adults journeying in faith' (page 74)

Reflecting on the theme

Living the theme ——————— see Family Sheet

At home

- Explain what the children are doing with their teacher/catechist and how parents can support this.
- Developing the 'Signs of Readiness'.
    Discuss with the parents who it is we are really saying 'sorry' to, and how to encourage the children to do so.
- Night Prayer: Prayer for the end of the day (using the Prayer Sheet).

At Mass

- Focus on the 'Our Father' – the prayer of all God's family.

Looking ahead

- Practicalities concerning   the next children's session
                                          the next parents' meeting.

Celebrating the theme

Explaining the liturgy – its purpose, what is being asked of the children and their families; practical planning.

Prayer

Using the resources, plan a closing prayer to reflect the theme of the session.

Closing the session

Thank the group for their participation.

Final words . . .

After the meeting

Tidying up and clarifying communication with families not represented at the meeting.

Team Preparation
Session 2: Planning sheet

1. Reviewing the last meeting

Questions for reflection   what went well?
with what were you disappointed?
what do you want to do differently?

2. Preparing yourselves

Share together your thoughts on 'Pause and reflect . . .'

3. Preparing for Session 2

Date _____ Time _____

Venue _____ Theme _____

Areas of responsibility	Team member
Publicity/reminder to parents of the next meeting	_____
Setting the scene	_____
Focal point	_____
Refreshments	_____
Welcome and introduction	_____
Leading into the theme	_____
Developing the theme	_____
Reflecting on the theme	_____
Living the theme	_____
Closing the session	_____
After the session – tidying up	_____
Contacting absent parents	_____

Resources

Family Sheet: what adaptations? _____

Worksheets/handouts to be duplicated _____

Page numbers: _____ _____

❏ Flipchart ❏ Felts ❏ Tape recorder _____

Session 2: Planning prayer

Focal point _____

Creating a mood of prayer
lighting a candle   yes/no
taped music   yes/no
taped song   yes/no

Invitation to pray

led by _____

Opening song/prayer

led by _____

Reading   with/without music backing
              with/without slides

Pause for reflection   with/without invitation to reread passage
                           with/without invitation to pick out keywords/phrases

Invitation to share reflection

led by _____

Invitation to share intentions

led by _____

Closing words/song

led by _____

Session 2: Pause and reflect

As you read and reflect on this passage, think back to your childhood images of God. How different are they now? What has changed them?

UNCLE GEORGE

God was a family relative, much admired by Mum and Dad, who described him as very loving, a great friend of the family, very powerful and interested in all of us. Eventually we are taken to visit 'Good Old Uncle George'. He lives in a formidable mansion, is bearded, gruff and threatening. We cannot share our parents' professed admiration for this jewel in the family. At the end of the visit, Uncle George turns to address us. 'Now listen, dear,' he begins, looking very severe, 'I want to see you here once a week, and if you fail to come, let me just show you what will happen to you.' He then leads us down to the mansion's basement. It is dark, becomes hotter and hotter as we descend, and we begin to hear unearthly screams. In the basement there are steel doors. Uncle George opens one. 'Now look in there, dear,' he says. We see a nightmare vision, an array of blazing furnaces with little demons in attendance, who hurl into the blaze those men, women and children who failed to visit Uncle George or to act in a way he approved. 'And if you don't visit me, dear, that is where you will most certainly go,' says Uncle George. He then takes us upstairs again to meet Mum and Dad. As we go home, tightly clutching Dad with one hand and Mum with the other, Mum leans over us and says, 'And don't you love Uncle George with all your heart and soul, mind and strength?' And we, loathing the monster, say, 'Yes, I do,' because to say anything else would be to join the queue at the furnace. At a tender age religious schizophrenia has set in and we keep telling Uncle George how much we love him and how good he is and that we want to do only what pleases him. We observe what we are told are his wishes and dare not admit, even to ourselves, that we loathe him.

God of Surprises
Gerard W. Hughes SJ
Darton, Longman & Todd, 1985

Family Sheet and Session notes/handouts follow.

'You are precious in my eyes'

God Calling Us into Relationship

Preparing to Celebrate Reconciliation

One night a man had a dream. He dreamed he was walking along the beach with the Lord. Across the sky flashed scenes from his life. For each scene he noticed two sets of footprints in the sand. One belonged to him, and one to the Lord. When the last scene flashed before him he looked back at the footprints and noticed that at many times along the path there was only one set of footprints in the sand. He also noticed that this happened during the lowest and saddest times in his life. This really bothered him and he questioned the Lord: 'Lord, you said that once I decided to follow you, you would walk all the way with me, but I noticed that during the most troublesome moments of my life there was only one set of footprints. I don't understand why – when I most needed you, you deserted me!' The Lord replied: 'My precious one, my precious child, I love you and would never leave you. During your time of trial and suffering, when you see only one set of footprints, it was then that I carried you!'

Margaret Fishback Powers

Prayer for the end of the day

Think about all that has happened today, at home, at school, with your friends . . .

Think about the happy things that have happened . . .

Say 'Thank you' to God our Father.

Think about the times things have gone wrong today, and the times you have caused unhappiness . . .

Tell Jesus you are sorry.

Jesus,
I trust in your love and forgiveness.
I am sorry for all the wrong things I have done.
I am sorry for all the good things I have not done.
I want to love you with all my heart.
Amen.

Think about tomorrow . . .

Ask the Holy Spirit to help you make it a happy day for all the people you meet.

Amen.

At home

- See what you can do to support your child's teacher/catechist.

- Developing the 'Signs of Readiness'. Encourage each person in the family (including yourself!) to say 'sorry' when they have hurt or upset someone.

- Night prayer: Prayer for the end of the day.

At Mass

Encourage your child to join in the 'Our Father' – the prayer of all God's family.

Dates for the diary

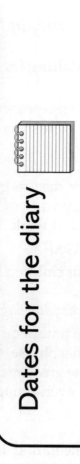

Have you ever thought of God in any of these ways?

*For Zion was saying, 'Yahweh has abandoned me,
the Lord has forgotten me'.
Does a woman forget her baby at the breast,
or fail to cherish the son of her womb?
Yet even if these forget, I will never forget you.
See I have branded you on the palms of my hands.*

(Isaiah 49:14-16)

What man among you with a hundred sheep, losing one, would not leave the ninety-nine in the wilderness and go after the missing one till he found it? And when he found it, would he not joyfully take it on his shoulders and then, when he got home, call together his friends and neighbours? 'Rejoice with me,' he would say, 'I have found my sheep that was lost.' In the same way, I tell you, there will be more rejoicing in heaven over one repentant sinner than over ninety-nine virtuous men who have no need of repentance.

(Luke 15:4-7)

Have you other images?

Who is the God you want your child to grow up knowing and loving?

*Do not be afraid, for I have redeemed you;
I have called you by your name, you are mine.
Should you pass through the sea, I will be with you;
or through rivers, they will not swallow you up.
Should you walk through fire, you will not be scorched
and the flames will not burn you.
For I am Yahweh, your God,
the Holy One of Israel, your saviour.*

*I give Egypt for your ransom,
and exchange Cush and Seba for you.
Because you are precious in my eyes,
because you are honoured and I love you.*

(Isaiah 43:1-3)

Adults journeying in faith – Catechists' notes

Introduce the theme: God – Calling Us into Relationship
A story
When my sister collected her four-year-old daughter at the end of her third day at school, young Ellie's opening words were, 'I'm never going to pray again in all my life'. The tears flowed . . .

When my sister asked Ellie why, she was greeted with the forceful response, 'It doesn't work. I prayed and prayed that you wouldn't be late and leave me all on my own in the playground again. It didn't work. You were late again. Prayer doesn't work.'
- What was Ellie's image of God?
- What image of God do your children have?

Invite the group to take part in the following exercise:
Close your eyes. Think of the times you have said to someone, 'I'm sorry'. Of the many times you have used this phrase, when did you mean it most deeply? How true would it be to say that the greater/deeper our relationship with someone, the deeper the level of sorrow – even though the event/action on the surface might seem fairly trivial?

- The absolute basis for celebrating this sacrament is relationship with God, awareness of who God is, and of God's unfailing, never ending love for me . . .

Leading into the theme: describe and explore
How we think of/envisage God
Using either the illustrated sheet or the selection of scripture quotations (pages 75 and 76), invite the parents
- to spend a few moments looking at/reading the sheet
- exchange thoughts and comments with their neighbour

Then invite a sharing of any reflections with the whole group, prompted by questions such as:
- Did any of you find you had chosen the same illustration/quotation?
- Have you thought of God in different ways during the different times of your life?
- What are some of the ways in which you want your child to see/know God?

Developing the theme: listen
Presenting some images of God we find in the scriptures, Church teachings and traditions (pages 77-79).

Reflecting on the theme: reflect and relate to life
Group discussion (page 80) allowing an opportunity for reflection on the presentation.

Have you ever thought of God in any of these ways?

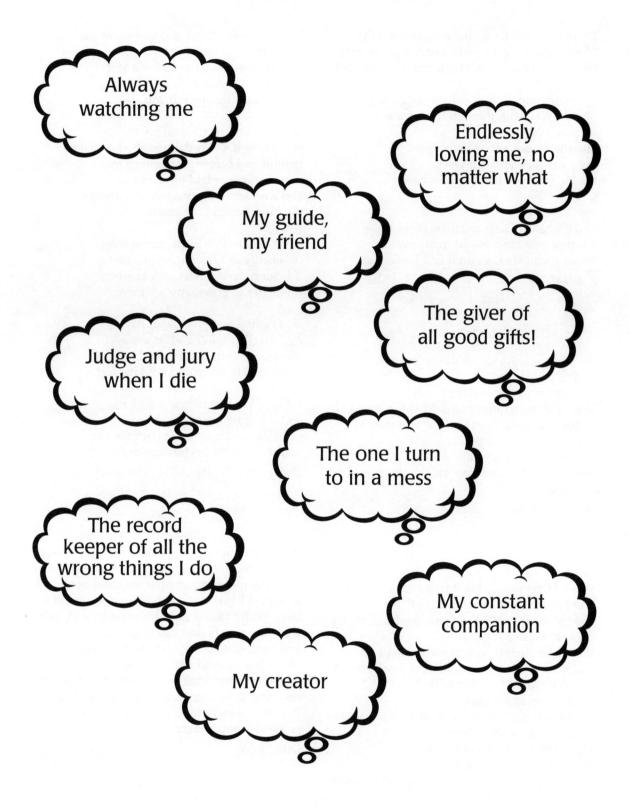

Have you other images?

Who is the God you want your child
to grow up knowing and loving?

Have you ever thought of God in any of these ways?

Do not be afraid, for I have redeemed you;
I have called you by your name, you are mine.
Should you pass through the sea, I will be with
   you;
or through rivers, they will not swallow you up.
Should you walk through fire, you will not be
   scorched
and the flames will not burn you.
For I am Yahweh, your God,
the Holy One of Israel, your saviour.

I give Egypt for your ransom,
and exchange Cush and Seba for you.
Because you are precious in my eyes,
because you are honoured and I love you.

Isaiah 43:1-3

For Zion was saying, 'Yahweh has abandoned
   me,
the Lord has forgotten me'.
Does a woman forget her baby at the breast,
or fail to cherish the son of her womb?
Yet even if these forget,
I will never forget you.
See I have branded you on the palms of my
   hands.

Isaiah 49:14-16

When Israel was a child I loved him,
and I called my son out of Egypt.
But the more I called to them, the further they
   went from me;
they have offered sacrifice to the Baals
and set their offerings smoking before the idols.
I myself taught Ephraim to walk,
I took them in my arms;
yet they have not understood that I was the
   one looking after them.
I led them with reins of kindness,
with leading-strings of love.
I was like someone who lifts an infant close
   against his cheek;
stooping down to him I gave him his food.

Hosea 11:1-4

Lord, you search me and you know me
you know my resting and my rising,
you discern my purpose from afar.
You mark when I walk or lie down,
all my ways lie open to you.

Before ever a word is on my tongue
you know it, O Lord, through and through.
Behind and before you besiege me,
your hand ever laid upon me.
Too wonderful for me, this knowledge,
too high, beyond my reach.

O where can I go from your spirit,
or where can I flee from you face?
If I climb the heavens, you are there.
If I lie in the grave, you are there.

If I take the wings of the dawn
and dwell at the sea's furthest end,
even there your hand would lead me,
your right hand would hold me fast.

If I say: 'Let the darkness hide me
and the light around me be night,'
even the darkness is not dark for you
and the night is as clear as the day.

Psalm 139:1-12 [Psalm 138, The Grail]

What man among you with a hundred sheep,
losing one, would not leave the ninety-nine in
the wilderness and go after the missing one till
he found it? And when he found it, would he
not joyfully take it on his shoulders and then,
when he got home, call together his friends
and neighbours? 'Rejoice with me,' he would
say. 'I have found my sheep that was lost.' In
the same way, I tell you, there will be more
rejoicing in heaven over one repentant sinner
than over ninety-nine virtuous men who have
no need of repentance.

Luke 15:4-7

Have you other images?

Who is the God you want your child to grow up knowing and loving?

A reflection on God – a presentation

Recently I spent the best part of three hours in the back of a car with my three-year-old great-nephew. To say I was exhausted by the time we reached our destination would be an understatement. Not having children of my own I had no idea how wearing incessant questioning can be. What's that man doing? What do you mean? Are we nearly there? Where's my mummy? They come thick and fast, each demanding an answer, or so I thought; wiser people, parents perhaps, turn a deaf ear and happily refuse to answer.

A child's question, however, can often put us on the spot. For example we might frequently use a particular word or phrase and it is only when someone asks what we mean by it that we can find ourselves struggling to answer. The more abstract the idea the more difficult the response. Take the word 'God'. Most of us use the word daily, perhaps in a morning offering or an act of contrition at night, sometimes in exhortation, even as an expression of exasperation. But what do we mean by the word? When we use it what images, thoughts, ideas, pictures come to mind? From where did we get these pictures and images? Have they changed as we have got older? Which are the ones we find most helpful today? Do we find it easy or difficult to articulate what we mean? Can we share our ideas with others or do we keep them locked up inside our own heads and hearts?

It can help to take a journey back in time, trying to remember our very first thoughts and images. I was born the youngest of seven children. My mother was the Catholic, my father was not. My first images came from my mother and the picture she gave me was of a God who was very nice and kind and who always wanted what was best for me. Then I went to school and was introduced to the Catechism and I learned by heart words about God which I didn't understand. God was the 'supreme being', not a lot of help to a child of six. But worse was to follow, because with the Catechism came the questions, and wrong answers brought instant punishment. Then I made my first confession and was introduced to a God who was pleased with me when I was good, but was unhappy with me when I was naughty. Quite where Jesus fitted into the picture I was not sure!

All of us will have our first memories and it is good to explore them, whether they are connected to a picture or a statue, a story from the Bible or a word from a parent or friend. Our chief source of information about God comes from the Bible: the Old Testament, which we share with the Jewish people and the New Testament, which tells us about Jesus Christ.

In the very first verses of the first book of the Old Testament, the Book of Genesis, we see God as the Creator – the creator of land and sea, night and day, animals, trees, plants and finally man and woman, created in God's own likeness. After each creation there is the refrain, 'And God saw that it was good'. Goodness, familiarity, wholeness, integrity, humankind at one with God – and God saw that it was good. But then, only a few verses later, we have the story of the Fall, and the very first human emotion mentioned in the Bible is 'fear'. Remember the story? God had told the man and woman to stay away from the tree in the middle of the garden, but then the serpent came and first the woman and then the man ate of the fruit of that tree. In the evening God was walking in the garden and he called to the man, who answered: 'I heard your voice in the garden and I was afraid because I was naked, so I hid'. I was afraid!

Fear has coloured so many people's image and picture of God. Not the 'fear of the Lord' which is a gift of the Holy Spirit, but a fear which breaks relationships, which puts distance between people, which means that we cannot respond properly. Despite the fact that we have more knowledge than any generation before us, that we can travel the world in comfort and at speed, many people's image of God is based on fear. God as the Judge waiting to pass sentence on my life, weighing the sins against the good; God as the unmarked policeman waiting to catch me out and give me a punishment; God as the person behind the net curtain watching my every move without my seeing. How often have we heard others, perhaps ourselves, saying, 'I knew God would do that'. It is good to check out our own, and other people's fears about God.

But there are other images in the Old Testament. Remember Abraham, called by God to leave his country and journey to another, unknown place. Abraham was married to Sarah and they were childless and, in human terms, past the age of childbearing. But God had different plans and eventually Sarah gave birth to Isaac. Perhaps only parents who have waited years to have a child can really appreciate how they must have felt, the rest of us can only imagine. And then God asked the ultimate of Abraham and Sarah, God wanted Isaac to be sacrificed. Abraham obeyed and was about to kill his son with a knife when an angel of the Lord told him to stop, he had proved his obedience to God's will. We call Abraham 'our father in faith' but what image of God comes from this story? Have there been times when we feel that God has asked too much of us? Are there times when we look at the world with its natural disasters and human tragedies and ask, 'How can God let this happen?' Is our faith tested when we watch a child die of cancer or an elderly person stricken with Alzheimer's disease? Are there times when the only prayer we can say is 'help' and the only question we can ask is 'why?'

And then we come to the prophets, people like Isaiah and Jeremiah, Ezekiel and Amos. They had the most unenviable task of speaking the truth to people who would prefer to listen to lies, asking those around them to open their eyes and see the error of their ways. God used the prophets to help the people understand that whatever misfortune they were experiencing, whatever suffering they were enduring, God was still with them. And furthermore, God would enter into human experience in a way that would be unique. And the people waited, and generations passed as the centuries went by until the moment came and 'The Word was made Flesh'.

With the life, death and resurrection of Jesus we get new insights into who God is. Jesus, to quote one author, is 'The Self Portrait by God'. If we want to know who God is we can do no better than deepen our knowledge of and our relationship with Jesus Christ. In parable and miracle, in word and deed, Jesus shows us the God in whom we believe and whose life we are called to share. Jesus' God is the owner of the vineyard who is generous to a fault, giving those who worked only one hour the same as those who worked the whole day, reminding us that our understanding of equality and fair play falls woefully short of God's. Jesus' God is a woman who sweeps the house clean until she finds the lost coin and when she does she invites others to share her joy. Jesus' God is a shepherd who leaves the ninety-nine sheep and goes in search of the one who strays, and on finding the lost sheep returns and celebrates with others. Jesus' God is the Prodigal Father who lets his son go, giving him the freedom to make mistakes, but who then looks out for him and runs to meet him when he returns, kissing him, giving him the symbols of sonship with robe and ring, ordering a feast, a celebration because 'this son of mine was lost and is found, was dead and has come to life'.

The God revealed by Jesus reaches out to those regarded as unclean, whether through sickness or social standing. The God revealed by Jesus chooses those whom others would regard as inadequate or inappropriate. The God revealed by Jesus gives a list of priorities which turns society's values upside down. It really doesn't matter how clever we are, what job we have, how much we possess. It really doesn't matter what strings we can pull, how important others think we are, what our social status is. The God revealed by Jesus tells us that what is ultimately important is the quality of our love, our love for God and our love for one another. The God revealed by Jesus loves each one of us uniquely and will never stop loving us no matter what we do or don't do. 'Nothing,' St Paul tells us, 'can separate us from the love of God made manifest in Christ Jesus.' Nothing at all, because God's love for us is unconditional.

So, pondering on the God revealed by Jesus in the Gospels, and reflected by St Paul and the other New Testament writers in the other letters, what images of God do we have? And what images of God do we want to share with others?

Bernard Bickers

For discussion

Of all that you have heard, has anything
- surprised you?
- pleased you?
- raised questions?

Sometimes things happen in life that make us question God:
- illness or the death of someone we love . . .
- earthquakes, famines . . .
- war, acts of terrorism . . .
- marriage breaking up . . .

When children ask, 'Why does God let . . .?', how can we respond?

What are some of the practical things we can do
- at home
- at school
- in the parish

to help our children to deepen their relationship with God?

From birth to death we are invited to deepen our relationship with God. Are there ways in which the parish can help us as adults to deepen our relationship with God?

> Thou has made us,
> O Lord, for thyself
> and our heart shall find no rest
> till it rest in thee.
> *St Augustine*

Session 3. 'I did not come to call the virtuous, but sinners'

Sin – Weakening/Breaking Our Relationship

General outline

Preparing the session

Focal point

Symbols/pictures reflecting the theme of the session,
e.g. something broken, a candle snuffed out.

Welcome

Welcome the group. Opening prayer. Invite the parents to introduce themselves to the person sitting on either side. Introduce the team, explain the plan of tonight's meeting and how it fits into the overall programme. Invite the parents to share any comments, reflections, since the last meeting – on the liturgy, what they have been doing at home . . .

Leading into the theme

Developing the theme ———————> see 'Adults journeying in faith' (page 90)

Reflecting on the theme

Living the theme ——————————— see Family Sheet

At home

- Explain what the children are doing with their teacher/catechist and how parents can support this.

- Developing the 'Signs of Readiness'.
    In addition to the emphasis on saying sorry, discuss with parents how they can look for opportunities to encourage their child to forgive others when they say sorry, or even if they don't.
    They can encourage their child to take responsibility for their actions, rather than blaming others. Affirm them when they do so.

- Night prayer: Prayer for the end of the day.

At Mass

Focus on the Penitential Rite: at the beginning of Mass we acknowledge we are sinners and ask for God's forgiveness, similarly with the 'Lamb of God . . .'

Looking ahead

- Practicalities concerning   the next children's session
                            the next parents' meeting.

Celebrating the theme
Explaining the Liturgy – its purpose, what is being asked of the children and their families; practical planning.

Prayer
Using the resources offered, plan a closing prayer to reflect the theme of the session.

Closing the session
Thank the group for their participation.
Final words . . .

After the meeting
Tidying up and clarifying communication for families not represented at the meeting.

Team preparation
Session 3: Planning sheet

1. Reviewing the last meeting

Questions for reflection   what went well?
with what were you disappointed?
what do you want to do differently?

2. Preparing yourselves

Share together your thoughts on 'Pause and reflect . . .'

3. Preparing for Session 3

Date _____ Time _____

Venue _____ Theme _____

Areas of responsibility	**Team member**
Publicity/reminder to parents of the next meeting	_____
Setting the scene	_____
Focal point	_____
Refreshments	_____
Welcome and introduction	_____
Leading into the theme	_____
Developing the theme	_____
Reflecting on the theme	_____
Living the theme	_____
Closing the session	_____
After the session – tidying up	_____
Contacting absent parents	_____

Resources

Family Sheet: what adaptations? _____

Worksheets/handouts to be duplicated _____

Page numbers: _____ _____

❑ Flipchart   ❑ Felts   ❑ Tape recorder _____

Session 3: Planning prayer

Focal point _____

Creating a mood of prayer
lighting a candle   yes/no
taped music   yes/no
taped song   yes/no

Invitation to pray

led by _____

Opening song/prayer

led by _____

Reading   with/without music backing
              with/without slides

Pause for reflection   with/without invitation to reread passage
                           with/without invitation to pick out keywords/phrases

Invitation to share reflection

led by _____

Invitation to share intentions

led by _____

Closing words/song

led by _____

Session 3: Pause and reflect, 1

As you meditate on this Eucharistic Prayer for Reconciliation, what reflections do you have on sin?

EUCHARISTIC PRAYER FOR RECONCILIATION II

Father, all-powerful and ever-living God,
we praise and thank you through Jesus Christ
    our Lord
for your presence and action in the world.

In the midst of conflict and division,
we know it is you
who turn our minds to thoughts of peace.
Your Spirit changes our hearts:
enemies begin to speak to one another,
those who were estranged join hands in
    friendship,
and nations seek the way of peace together.

Your Spirit is at work
when understanding puts an end to strife,
when hatred is quenched by mercy,
and vengeance gives way to forgiveness.

For this we should never cease
to thank and praise you.
We join with all the choirs of heaven
as they sing for ever to your glory:

Holy, holy, holy Lord, God of power and might.
Heaven and earth are full of your glory.
Hosanna in the highest.
Blessed is he who comes in the name of the
    Lord.
Hosanna in the highest.

God of power and might,
we praise you through your Son, Jesus Christ,
who comes in your name.
He is the Word that brings salvation.
He is the hand you stretch out to sinners.
He is the way that leads to your peace.

Therefore we celebrate the reconciliation
Christ has gained for us.

We ask you to sanctify these gifts
by the power of your Spirit,
as we now fulfil your Son's command.

While he was at supper
on the night before he died for us,
he took bread in his hands,
and gave you thanks and praise.
He broke the bread,
gave it to his disciples, and said:

Take this, all of you and eat it:
this is my body which will be given up for you.

At the end of the meal he took the cup.

Again he praised you for your goodness,
and gave the cup to his disciples, and said:

Take this, all of you, and drink from it:
this is the cup of my blood,
the blood of the new and everlasting covenant.
It will be shed for you and for all
so that sins may be forgiven.
Do this in memory of me.

Let us proclaim the mystery of faith:

Lord, by your cross and resurrection
you have set us free.
You are the Saviour of the world.

Lord, our God,
your Son has entrusted to us
this pledge of his love.
We celebrate the memory of his death and
    resurrection
and bring you the gift you have given us,
the sacrifice of reconciliation.
Therefore, we ask you, Father,
to accept us, together with your Son.

Fill us with his Spirit
through our sharing in this meal.
May he take away all that divides us.

May this Spirit keep us always in communion
with N . . ., our pope, N . . ., our bishop (and his
    assistant bishops),
with all the bishops and all your people.
Father, make your Church throughout the world
a sign of unity and an instrument of your peace.

You have gathered us here
around the table of your Son,
in fellowship with the Virgin Mary,
Mother of God, and all the saints.

In that new world where the fullness of your
    peace will be revealed,
gather people of every race, language,
    and way of life
to share in the one eternal banquet
with Jesus Christ the Lord.

Through him,
with him,
in him,
in the unity of the Holy Spirit,
all glory and honour is yours,
almighty Father,
for ever and ever. Amen.   ICEL

Session 3: Pause and reflect, 2
As you read this passage, what reflections on sin does it stir?

REPENTANCE

Now as a person tries to practise the repentance without ceasing, inside and outside of prayer, they are open at all times to the divine love that brings our poor human attempts at loving to perfection. Archbishop Arnou described so well how this process works inside of prayer. But let me tell you a story from Africa, to show you how the same process works outside of prayer. It was a remarkable story, told to me by a young African Sister when I was working in Uganda. It all began with a horrifying experience that she had to endure while on home leave with her family. A band of marauding cattle rustlers from a neighbouring tribe came across the border from Kenya, and brutally attacked her family. Her father was hacked to death with machetes before her eyes, and then she had to watch as her four brothers were used as target practice by the invaders until they were all speared to death. Her mother fled into the bush where she simply went out of her mind. She is now being looked after in a missionary hospital, but there is nothing that can be done for her. She has reverted to the days of her early motherhood, and spends her time nursing her four imaginary sons whom she will never see again.

Two years after the terrible killings took place, the Sister was walking through a ward in the hospital where she had been assigned, when she saw in one of the beds the leader of the gang who had massacred her family. She told me that she didn't know how she managed to continue walking, because it was as if some awful paralysis took hold of her, and all but prevented her from moving. The Sister on the ward said the man was dying from stab wounds inflicted upon him by some cattle thieves who attacked his own home. He couldn't speak properly because a spear had pierced his neck. For six days the man lingered on in terrible pain, and each day the Sister had to walk through the ward on the way to her own. She said that despite the wounds and the terrible pain he was obviously undergoing, she could feel nothing but hatred for the man, and she even took sadistic delight in knowing that at last he was getting his just desserts. But as the days went by, her conscience began to prick her until one morning the man suddenly noticed and recognised her.

From then on he tried to cry out to her each day as she passed the end of his bed. She knew what he wanted, but she said forgiveness was the one thing she couldn't give him, not after what he had done to her family. Then one night she tossed and turned in bed till dawn without getting a wink of sleep. She knew she ought to love her enemies, for the Gospel was quite clear about it, but she simply couldn't. In no way could she forgive that man. Then she suddenly realised that she was living a lie, dressed up as a disciple of a man whose life and example she could not follow.

At odd moments she did try to pray for strength to do what she knew she ought to do, but she felt it was hopeless. As she entered the man's ward the next day, he saw her the moment she came in, and started to make pathetic noises to attract her attention, for he couldn't speak. She looked straight ahead and pretended not to notice him, but when she came to the bottom of his bed she felt that she had to do something. 'I couldn't love him, that's for sure,' she said to herself. 'No way can I forgive that man, but I must do what I can. My heart is like a heavy stone and it's quite immovable. I simply can't move it no matter what, but at least I can move my hand.' And so she walked over and stood by his bed. Mechanically she raised her hand and put it into his. Then, she said, as her hand was being placed into his, something happened inside; something happened to soften that heart of stone, for she suddenly experienced a deep love welling up from within, reaching out to that dying man, and then, before she knew what was happening, she bent over and kissed him on the forehead. It was a kiss of genuine Christ-like love. It was a kiss of real and heartfelt forgiveness, that she knew she was quite incapable of performing.

She had no illusions about what happened. She didn't love him; she didn't forgive him. It was Another working through her that gave her the gift she so desperately desired, but which she alone was quite incapable of performing.

From *The Prophet*
David Torkington
Mercier Press, Cork

See following pages for Family Sheet and Session notes/handouts.

'I did not come to call the virtuous, but sinners'

Sin – Weakening/Breaking our Relationship

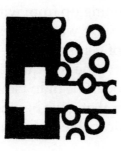

Preparing to celebrate Reconciliation

Part of being human is to struggle with sin; even St Paul had this struggle . . . .

I cannot understand my own behaviour. I fail to carry out the things I want to do, and I find myself doing the very things I hate.
Romans 7:15

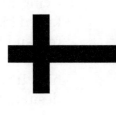

Prayer for the end of the day

Think about all that has happened today, at home, at school, with your friends . . .

Think about the happy things that have happened . . .

Say 'Thank you' to God our Father.

Think about the times things have gone wrong today, and the times you have caused unhappiness . . .

Tell Jesus you are sorry.

Jesus
I trust in your love and forgiveness.
I am sorry for all the wrong things I have done.
I am sorry for all the good things I have not done.
I want to love you with all my heart.
Amen.

Think about tomorrow . . . .

Ask the Holy Spirit to help you make it a happy day for all the people you meet.

Amen.

At home

- See what you can do to support your child's teacher/catechist.
- Developing the 'Signs of Readiness'.

In addition to the emphasis on saying 'sorry', look for opportunities to encourage your child to forgive others when they say 'sorry', or even if they don't. Affirm them when they do!

Encourage your child to take responsibility for their actions rather than blaming others.

- Night prayer: Prayer for the end of the day.

At Mass

Join in the Penitential Rite: at the beginning of Mass we acknowledge we are sinners and ask for God's forgiveness: I confess . . .; Lord, have mercy . . .

Dates for the diary

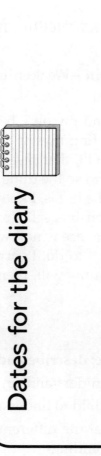

What is sin?

Every day we make all sorts of choices, some right, some wrong.

- When I choose to put myself first at the expense of others – it can lead to sin.

- When I choose to go against what I know is right – it can lead to sin.

- When I choose to ignore the place of God in my life – it can lead to sin.

- When I choose to ignore the needs of others – it can lead to sin.

Sin is when I choose to walk away from God – the God who gives me life.

THERE IS A WAY which seems right to man, but in the end, it leads to death...

LIFE   DEATH

Phooey! I'm doing it *my way!*

Adults journeying in faith – Catechists' notes

Introduce the theme: Sin – Weakening/Breaking our Relationship

A reflection from St Paul:

> I cannot understand my own behaviour. I fail to carry out the things I want to do, and I find myself doing the very things I hate. When I act against my own will, that means I have a self that acknowledges that the law is good, and so the thing behaving in that way is not myself but sin living in me. The fact is, I know of nothing good living in me – living, that is, in my unspiritual self – for though the will to do what is good is in me, the performance is not, with the result that instead of doing the good things I want to do, I carry out the sinful things I do not want. When I act against my will, then, it is not my true self doing it, but sin which lives in me.
>
> *Romans 7:15-20*

Leading into the theme: describe and explore

- How do I describe/understand sin?
- How do I want my child to understand sin?

Invite parents to look at the different definitions of sin (page 91) and see which echo their own understanding.

    or

Invite parents to work in twos, sharing their definitions of sin (page 92). Each couple could compare their definitions with another couple. Invite feedback and list the definitions on a flipchart.

Developing the theme: listen

Some reflections on sin from the scriptures, Church teachings and traditions.

- Invite parents to look at the scripture quotations (page 93). What do these tell us of Jesus' attitude towards sinners?
- Using the notes provided (pages 94 and 95), or having prepared your own presentation, invite the parents to consider how the Church explains sin.

Reflecting on the theme: reflect and relate to life

Group discussion (page 96) allowing for an opportunity for reflection on the presentation (pages 94 and 95).

What is sin?

Offending God?

Missing the mark?

Disobeying the law?

Hardness of heart?

Failing to use my talents and abilities, not living up to my full human potential?

An attitude?

A sort of evil force deep inside us?

'Those things I want to do, those I do not, those things I do not want to do, those I do?'

Selfishness?

Being stiff-necked?

Refusing to carry that daily cross?

Which of these descriptions echoes your understanding of sin?

Self-centredness?

A frame of mind?

Offending God and the community?

Failing to love?

Anything that brings about disharmony in life?

The breaking of a relationship between myself and God or myself and my neighbour?

Not doing the good thing that is obviously called for?

Individual acts?

I seem to be able to resist everything but temptation . . .

The failure to rejoice in the person I am or am called to be?

And as he sat at table in his house, many tax collectors and sinners were sitting with Jesus and his disciples; for there were many who followed him. And the scribes of the Pharisees, when they saw that he was eating with sinners and tax collectors, said to his disciples, 'Why does he eat with tax collectors and sinners?' And when Jesus heard it, he said to them, 'Those who are well have no need of a physician, but those who are sick; I came not to call the righteous, but sinners.' *Mark 2:15-17 RSV*

Now the tax collectors and sinners were all drawing near to hear him. And the Pharisees and the scribes murmured, saying, 'This man receives sinners and eats with them.'

So he told them this parable: 'What man of you, having a hundred sheep, if he has lost one of them, does not leave the ninety-nine in the wilderness, and go after the one which is lost, until he finds it? And when he has found it, he lays it on his shoulders, rejoicing. And when he comes home, he calls together his friends and his neighbours, saying to them, "Rejoice with me, for I have found my sheep which was lost." Just so, I tell you, there will be more joy in heaven over one sinner who repents than over ninety-nine righteous persons who need no repentance.' *Luke 15:1-7 RSV*

And many were gathered together, so that there was no longer room for them, not even about the door; and he was preaching the word to them. And they came, bringing to him a paralytic carried by four men. And when they could not get near him because of the crowd, they removed the roof above him; and when they had made an opening, they let down the pallet on which the paralytic lay. And when Jesus saw their faith, he said to the paralytic, 'My son, your sins are forgiven.'

Now some of the scribes were sitting there, questioning in their hearts, 'Why does this man speak thus? It is blasphemy! Who can forgive sins but God alone?' and immediately Jesus, perceiving in his spirit that they thus questioned within themselves, said to them, 'Why do you question thus in your hearts? Which is easier, to say to the paralytic, "Your sins are forgiven," or to say, "Rise, take up your pallet and walk"? But that you may know that the Son of man has authority on earth to forgive sins' – he said to the paralytic – 'I say to you, rise, take up your pallet and go home.' And he rose, and immediately took up the pallet and went out before them all; so that they were all amazed and glorified God, saying, 'We never saw anything like this!' *Mark 2: 2-12 RSV*

A reflection on sin – a presentation

'Sorry, I shouldn't have said that!' 'Sorry, I shouldn't have done that!' 'Sorry, I didn't mean to . . .' 'Sorry' is a word we know only too well. Perhaps we have to say it quite a lot to those we love the most, perhaps other people say it to us. Sometimes we find it difficult to say because we don't feel able to ask the other person for forgiveness, and sometimes we don't want to hear the word because we are unable or unwilling to forgive the one who has hurt or upset us. As children grow and develop and begin to know what they can and cannot do, 'sorry' enters their vocabulary as well. 'You know you shouldn't do that, say you're sorry and we'll forget all about it.'

Earlier we reflected on our understanding of God and we acknowledged that we carry with us all sorts of ideas about God which were given to us in our own childhood. The authors of the Book of Genesis, the very first book in the Bible, also reflected on God and on humankind's relationship with God. They recognised that in the beginning man and woman were created in God's image and likeness, that they shared an intimacy with God. But their own experience was very different. They experienced a separation from God, they experienced pain and suffering, they experienced hardship, alienation and death. Reflecting on this experience, they understood the change to have come about through sin, the sin of disobedience when the man and woman refused to listen to God's word but followed that of another, and far from becoming like gods, they were ashamed and afraid and lost their innocence and their intimacy with God. They became, as we say in the prayer *Hail The Holy Queen*, 'the poor banished children of Eve'.

Sin enters the story in the Bible very early and it has been part of human experience ever since. In the Bible sin means a refusal to listen to God and to listen to other voices, whether those are of our own making or come from others. Sin brings with itself a feeling of disorder and disharmony, because in its most violent forms it cuts us off from God who is the source of our life, and it affects others. In the Bible there is no such thing as a victimless sin, the sinner is always a victim, but so are others. Sin is like a stone being thrown into a pond, causing waves or ripples both on the surface and in the depths of the water. In the Bible sin is always something positive, something done, something evil which is brought into existence and continues in existence until it is wiped out and done away with. Sin always has consequences which we sometimes speak of in terms of guilt or punishment. In the Bible sin has a communal aspect, it is never simply a private affair between the individual and God.

As we turn the pages of the Old Testament we find a love story between God who is utterly faithful and a people who respond in different ways to God's love, sometimes faithfully and heroically, sometimes faithlessly and sinfully. In other words, among Jesus' ancestors were the great and the good but also the insignificant and the sinner. The Prophets constantly call the people back to God, to repent of their sin, to change their ways, to acknowledge their mistakes, their wrong choices, their wrong turnings. And when we get to the life of Jesus, we find that among his first words are 'Repent and believe'. How many times do we hear the words 'Your sins are forgiven' on Jesus' lips? Think of the parables of forgiveness, most especially that of the Prodigal Son in Luke, chapter 15. At the heart of our faith is the belief that Jesus' life, death and resurrection have restored our intimacy with God and have destroyed sin and death for ever.

But we also know that St John tells us that if we think we have no sin in us then we are deceiving ourselves. Sin is part of the human condition and our whole lives are spent in a constant tug of war against it. We live in a society which has structures which are sinful in that they keep other people in poverty or under the burden of impossible debt. We have the power of advertising which prompts us always to be wanting more. Everything around us tells us not to mend what is broken but to go out and buy what is new. The emphasis today is on 'me', the individual, on what I want. It is a very short step to dismissing the needs and wants of others and to plunging into utter selfishness.

There are many ways of saying sorry for our sins, an Act of Contrition at the end of the day as part of our night prayer; the Penitential Rite at the beginning of Mass, and of course the Sacrament of Reconciliation which is now offered to us in three different rites. To make the most of any or all of these ways we need first to acknowledge our sins, and that takes honesty and humility. Then we need to say sorry and ask forgiveness of God, which we know is there. Finally we pray also for God's help and strength to move away from our sins whatever they are and to be more open to God's Word, a Word which brings us life. *God loved us with so much love that he was generous with his mercy. When we were dead through our sins he brought us to life in Christ and raised us up with him in heaven, in Christ Jesus* (Ephesians 2:4-6).

Bernard Bickers

For discussion

1. From all that you have heard,
   - what surprises you?
   - pleases you?
   - raises questions?

2. How has your understanding of sin changed since you were a child?

3. What understanding of sin can we expect a 7- or 8-year-old to have?
   What understanding do we want them to have?

4. How can we help our children to grow in their understanding of sin?

5. How can we help our children to grow in their awareness of God's never-ending love?

They were trying to guide us
to do right and be good,
and they didn't even know
what being good was.
When I was a little boy,
Mama and Dad would beat me
and tell me, 'You better be good,'
but I didn't know what being good was.
To me, it meant that they just wanted me
to sit down and fold my hands
or something crazy like that.
Stay in front of the house,
don't go anyplace,
don't get into trouble.
I didn't know what it meant,
and I don't think
they knew what it meant,
because they couldn't ever tell me
what they really wanted.

The way I saw it,
everything I was doing was good.
If I stole something
and didn't get caught,
I was good.
If I got into a fight with somebody
I tried to be good
and beat him.
If I broke into a place,
I tried to be quiet and steal
as much as I could. I was always trying to
be good.

'Trying To Be Good'
by Claude Brown
from *Listen to Love*
Louis Savary *et al*
Geoffrey Chapman, 1970

Session 4. 'He was lost and is found' _____

Reconciliation – Renewing Our Relationship

General outline

Preparing the session
Focal point
Symbols/pictures reflecting the theme of the session,
e.g. large poster of Rembrandt's *Return of the Prodigal Son*.

Welcome
Welcome the group. Opening prayer. Invite the parents to introduce themselves to the person sitting on either side. Introduce the team, explain the plan of tonight's meeting and how it fits into the overall programme. Invite the parents to share any comments, reflections since the last meeting – on the liturgy, home activities, the children's readiness to celebrate the sacrament.

Leading into the theme

Developing the theme 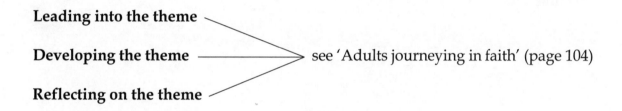 see 'Adults journeying in faith' (page 104)

Reflecting on the theme

Living the theme ——————— see Family Sheet
At home

- Explain what the children are doing with their teacher/catechist and how parents can support this.

- Developing the 'Signs of Readiness'.
  Discuss with parents how in addition to the emphasis on saying sorry, forgiving others and taking responsibility for personal actions rather than blaming others, they can encourage their child to control him- or herself, e.g. temper. Share some of the struggles you have doing this!
  They can help their child to understand that a small thing done on purpose is more serious than a larger 'catastrophe' caused by accident . . .

- Night prayer: Prayer for the end of the day.

At Mass
- Focus on the Sign of Peace as well as the 'Our Father' and Penitential Rite.

Looking ahead
- Practicalities concerning the context of
  a. the celebration of the sacrament
  b. the parish First Holy Communion programme

Celebrating the theme

Explain in detail the Reconciliation Service where the children will be celebrating the sacrament, the role of the parents and any practicalities concerning the liturgy (pages 115-117). It might be helpful to remind parents of the three rites/ways of celebrating this sacrament (page 60).

Explore how this can be the first of many celebrations of the sacrament – or the last?

Prayer

Using the resources, plan a closing prayer to reflect the theme of the session.

Closing the session

Thank the group for their participation.
Final words . . .

After the meeting

Tidying up and clarifying communication with families not represented at the meeting.

Team preparation
Session 4: Planning sheet

1. Reviewing the last meeting

Questions for reflection   what went well?
with what were you disappointed?
what do you want to do differently?

2. Preparing yourselves

Share together your thoughts on 'Pause and reflect . . .'

3. Preparing for Session 4

Date _____ Time _____

Venue _____ Theme _____

Areas of responsibility	**Team member**
Publicity/reminder to parents of the next meeting	_____
Setting the scene	_____
Focal point	_____
Refreshments	_____
Welcome and introduction	_____
Leading into the theme	_____
Developing the theme	_____
Reflecting on the theme	_____
Living the theme	_____
Closing the session	_____
After the session – tidying up	_____
Contacting absent parents	_____

Resources

Family Sheet: what adaptations? _____

Worksheets/handouts to be duplicated _____

Page numbers: _____ _____

❑ Flipchart   ❑ Felts   ❑ Tape recorder _____

Session 4: Planning prayer

Focal point _____

Creating a mood of prayer
lighting a candle   yes/no
taped music   yes/no
taped song   yes/no

Invitation to pray

led by _____

Opening song/prayer

led by _____

Reading   with/without music backing
            with/without slides

Pause for reflection   with/without invitation to reread passage
                        with/without invitation to pick out keywords/phrases

Invitation to share reflection

led by _____

Invitation to share intentions

led by _____

Closing words/song

led by _____

Session 4: Pause and reflect

Spend some time quietly reading and reflecting on the passage.
What does it say to you about sin and forgiveness?

I have fallen, Lord,
once more.
I can't go on, I'll never succeed.
I am ashamed, I don't dare look at you.
And yet I struggled, Lord, for I knew
you were right near me, bending over
    me, watching.
But temptation blew like a hurricane
and instead of looking at you I turned
    my head away.
I stepped aside
while you stood, silent and sorrowful,
like the spurned fiancé who sees his
    loved one carried off by his rival.
When the wind died down as suddenly
    as it had arisen,
when the lightning ceased after proudly
    streaking the darkness,
all of a sudden I found myself alone,
    ashamed, disgusted, with my sin in
    my hands.
I can't get rid of it.
I run from it, like the master
    of an unwanted and mangy dog,
    but it catches up with me,
and rubs joyfully against my legs.
Everyone must notice it.
I'm so ashamed that I feel like crawling
    to avoid being seen.
I'm ashamed of being seen by my
    friend,
I'm ashamed of being seen by you,
    Lord,
for you loved me, and I forgot you.

I forgot you because I was thinking of
    myself,
and one can't think of several persons
    at once.
One must choose, and I chose.
And your voice,
and your look,
and your love hurt me.
They weigh me down,
they weigh me down more than my sin.

Lord, don't look at me like that,
for I am naked,
I am dirty,
I am down,
shattered,
with no strength left.
I dare make no more promises, I can
    only stand bowed before you.

Come, son, look up.
Isn't it mainly your vanity that is
    wounded?
If you loved me, you would grieve,
    but you would trust.

Do you think that there's a limit to
    God's love?
Do you think that for a moment I
    stopped loving you?
But you still rely on yourself, son.
You must rely on me.

Ask my pardon
and get up quickly.
You see, it's not falling that is the worst,
but staying on the ground.

Prayers of Life, Michel Quoist
Gill & McMillan, 1963

101

'He was lost and is found'

Reconciliation –
Renewing Our Relationship

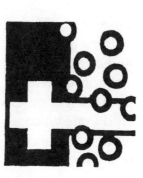

Preparing to celebrate Reconciliation

'But now, now – it is Yahweh who speaks –
come back to me with all your heart,
fasting, weeping, mourning.'
Let your hearts be broken,
not your garments torn,
turn to Yahweh your God again,
for he is all tenderness and compassion,
slow to anger, rich in graciousness,
and ready to relent.

Joel 2:12-13

Prayer for the end of the day

Think about all that has happened today, at home, at
school, with your friends . . .

Think about the happy things that have happened . . .

Say 'Thank you' to God our Father.

Think about the times things have gone wrong today,
and the times you have caused unhappiness . . .

Tell Jesus you are sorry.

Jesus
I trust in your love and forgiveness.
I am sorry for all the wrong things I have done.
I am sorry for all the good things I have not done.
I want to love you with all my heart.
Amen.

Think about tomorrow . . .

Ask the Holy Spirit to help you make it a happy day
for all the people you meet.

Amen.

At home

- See what you can do to support your child's teacher/catechist.
- Developing the 'Signs of Readiness'.
  In addition to the emphasis on saying 'sorry', forgiving others and taking responsibility for personal actions rather than blaming others, encourage your child to control his or her temper. Share some of the struggles you have doing this!
  Help your child to understand that a small thing done on purpose is more serious than a larger 'catastrophe' caused by accident . . .
- Night prayer: Prayer for the end of the day.

At Mass

- As well as the 'Our Father', the Penitential Rite, the Lamb of God, encourage your child to join in the Sign of Peace.

Note for Catechists:

As the celebration of the Sacrament of Reconciliation follows this meeting, you may need to discuss with the children's teacher/catechist what should be included here.

Family quiz on Confession

Some of the sentences below are true, some are false. Put a tick by the true ones and a cross by the false.

1. Confession gives us a chance to think about ourselves and how we are living.

2. We have to tell all our sins, everything we have done wrong on purpose.

3. We can trust the priest never to mention what we have told him in Confession.

4. When we hear the words of forgiveness, we can be sure we are forgiven if we are sorry.

5. We can, if we want, talk to the priest about things that worry us.

6. We must go to Confession once a month.

7. Confession helps us to make a fresh start.

8. We have to go to Confession every time we commit a sin.

9. Confession is about being sorry and being forgiven.

10. Sin is saying 'no' to loving other people.

11. Everybody struggles sometimes to live in God's way.

12. God our Father never stops loving us.

Compiled by Ruth Cardwell, *The Grail*

Adults journeying in faith – Catechists' notes

Introduce the theme: Reconciliation – Renewing our Relationship
A reflection

'But now, now – it is Yahweh who speaks – come back to me with all your heart, fasting, weeping, mourning.' Let your hearts be broken, not your garments torn, turn to Yahweh your God again, for he is all tenderness and compassion, slow to anger, rich in graciousness, and ready to relent (Joel 2:12-13).

or

An invitation to look at Rembrandt's *Return of the Prodigal Son.* What do you see? *Dimmed lights and candle-light highlight it* (page 105).

Leading into the theme: describe and explore
Choices

Invite the group to reflect on what choices they have made in the last twenty-four hours. Feedback, observations – some crucial, some not so important . . .

Introduce and read aloud the story of *The Return of the Prodigal Son* (pages 106-107). Invite parents to work in twos or threes, looking at who makes what choices in each section.

Work through the story, taking feedback, adding your own comments if necessary.

Developing the theme: listen

Share some reflections on the story (pages 108-112).

Reflecting on the theme: reflect and relate to life

Work through the story again, picking out the key points. We can look at ourselves in relation to the son.

The Son	*Me*
His relationship with the father	I am in relationship with God
a growing selfishness, going away from the father	I choose to live more selfishly
living totally selfishly	I sin
eventual misery because of that life, realisation that this is not life-giving, there is another way	I realise that deep down this is not the way I want to live
desire to return to the father	I want to put things right
sorrow and repentance	I am sorry, I want forgiveness
return	I go to Confession
acknowledgement of sin to the father	I acknowledge my sin
acceptance, forgiveness, reconciliation	I listen to words of healing and forgiveness
celebration	I thank God, do my penance
living as the father's son	I try to live in God's way

Explain how this relates to all three Rites of Reconciliation. Allow time for questioning, comments, discussion.

The Return of the Prodigal Son

An invaluable resource when reflecting on Rembrandt's *Return of the Prodigal Son* is Henri Nouwen's *The Return of the Prodigal Son* (Darton, Longman & Todd, 1992). These notes, adapted from Nouwen's book, might help to focus attention when meditating on the picture – or you could prepare your own notes.

The father	Looking at him, what words come to mind? What kind of person is he?
The hands	The left one: strong, muscular, fingers spread out covering a large part of the back/shoulders, not just touching but holding.
	The right one: refined, soft, tender, lies gently, wants to caress, to stroke, to comfort, a mother's touch.
	Does a woman forget her baby at the breast, or fail to cherish the child of her womb? Yet even if these forget I will never forget you. See, I have branded you on the palms of my hand. (Isaiah 49:15-16)
Red cloak/bent body	A sign of dignity and status, warm colour, tent shape. Welcoming place to be. Sheltering wings of a mother bird.
	Jerusalem, Jerusalem . . . how often have I longed to gather your children, as a hen gathers her chicks under her wings, and you refused. (Matthew 23:37)
The son	Looking at him, what words come to mind? What kind of person is he?
Shaven head	One of the signs of being robbed of individuality, e.g. in a prison or concentration camp.
Clothes	Underclothes covering an emaciated, undernourished body, a stark contrast to the father.
Feet	Soles tell of long, hard journey. The left foot scarred, on the right, the broken sandal, worn out, useless.
Sword	Remaining sign of his dignity, symbol of sonship. He hadn't forgotten he was the son of his father. That valued sonship brought him back.

The Lost Son (the 'Prodigal') Luke 15:11-32

What choices?

For whom?

The tax collectors and the sinners, meanwhile, were all seeking his company to hear what he had to say, and the Pharisees and the scribes complained. 'This man' they said 'welcomes sinners and eats with them.' So he spoke this parable to them:

'A man had two sons. The younger said to his father, "Father, let me have the share of the estate that would come to me." So the father divided the property between them. A few days later, the younger son got together everything he had and left for a distant country where he squandered his money on a life of debauchery.

What choices?

For whom?

What choices?

'When he had spent it all, that country experienced a severe famine, and now he began to feel the pinch, so he hired himself out to one of the local inhabitants who put him on his farm to feed the pigs. And he would willingly have filled his belly with the husks the pigs were eating but no one offered him anything. Then he came to his senses and said, "How many of my father's paid servants have more food than they want, and here am I dying of hunger! I will leave this place and go to my father and say: Father, I have sinned against heaven and against you; I no longer deserve to be called your son; treat me as one of your paid servants." So he left the place and went back to his father.

'While he was still a long way of, his father saw him and was moved with pity. He ran to the boy, clasped him in his arms and kissed him tenderly. Then his son said, "Father, I have sinned against heaven and against you. I no longer deserve to be called your son." But the father said to his servants, "Quick! Bring out the best robe and put it on him; put a ring on his finger and sandals on his feet. Bring the calf we have been fattening, and kill it; we are going to have a feast, a celebration, because this son of mine was dead and has come back to life; he was lost and is found." And they began to celebrate.

What choices?

What choices?
For whom?

'Now the elder son was out in the fields, and on his way back, as he drew near the house, he could hear music and dancing. Calling one of the servants he asked what it was all about. "Your brother has come," replied the servant "and your father has killed the calf we had fattened because he has got him back safe and sound." He was angry then and refused to go in, and his father came out to plead with him; but he answered his father, "Look, in all these years I have slaved for you and never once disobeyed your orders, yet you never offered me so much as a kid for me to celebrate with my friends. But, for this son of yours, when he comes back after swallowing up your property – he and his women – you kill the calf we had been fattening."

'The father said, "My son, you are with me always and all I have is yours. But it was only right we should celebrate and rejoice, because your brother here was dead and has come to life; he was lost and is found."'

A reflection on forgiveness – a presentation

The heart of Luke's gladdening news is contained in chapter 15. It can be viewed, I believe, as a summary of the Gospel; the Gospel in a nutshell. The theme of the chapter is heralded in the introductory description of the context in which Jesus finds himself.

> The tax collectors and sinners, however, were all crowding round to listen to him, and the Pharisees and scribes complained, saying, 'This man welcomes sinners and eats with them', (Luke 15:1-2).

At the outset we encounter a situation of division, as Simeon foretold (2:34-35). On the one hand, there are the 'tax collectors and sinners', the marginalised and religious outcasts. They are 'all' there, drawing close to Jesus. Luke is fond of the universal 'all'. The Greek may indicate that this was typical of his ministry and not simply a single incident. Their purpose is to listen to his words, a response to his injunction which precedes this narrative: 'Anyone who has ears for listening should listen!' (14:35). For Luke, a willingness to hear, to listen, is a sign of conversion.

On the other hand, there are the 'Pharisees and scribes', the exclusive religious elite who keep their distance to avoid contamination, and shun table fellowship with sinners. They 'grumble' repeatedly and openly (the imperfect of the intensive form of the verb is used), bringing to mind the complaining of the people against Moses in the wilderness. Their criticism is focused not only on Jesus' eating and drinking with these people (as in 5:30 and 7:34), but also on his welcoming them with acceptance, his offering hospitality. To host sinners would have been a more serious offence to the Pharisees than simply to eat with sinners informally or to accept invitations, which was itself scandalous enough.

In that culture, to share table was an offer of peace, trust, brotherhood and forgiveness; in short, sharing a table meant sharing life. Jesus' action in sharing meals is an expression of his mission and message. 'The inclusion of sinners in the community of salvation, achieved in table fellowship, is the most meaningful expression of the message of the redeeming love of God' (Jeremias in Bailey). It is itself a powerful parable of the Kingdom; it too is the Gospel in a nutshell.

Jesus seeks to justify and explain his attitude and conduct by recounting three parables; two short ones in tandem (the lost sheep and the lost coin), and the longer parable of the lost sons. The commonly used title, the 'Prodigal Son', is inaccurate and misleading. The parable is about two sons; the father has lost them both in different ways. The story describes the prodigality of the father, his extravagant love, as he seeks them both.

Opening

The younger son approaches his father one day and asks him for his portion of the estate, which would probably amount to a third of the property. To make such a request whilst the father is still alive is tantamount to wishing for his father's death. It is an extraordinary insult, something unheard of in such a culture. As long as the father lives, a son has no entitlement. 'The father demonstrates almost unbelievable love by granting the request.' This means that he has ownership, but no right to dispose of his share. The property belongs to him, but he can't sell it. The father normally had the right to live off the proceeds till he died. The son must have made a further demand, then, to sell his portion for ready cash immediately. The implication is: 'Father, I can't wait for you to die.' He wishes to sever the relationship utterly. And remarkably, very remarkably in that cultural context, the father agrees, jeopardising his own living and future, and thus showing an amazing quality of love, accepting rejection, and giving his son the freedom to go. He would also have to act as if he has decided to dispose of the property unpressurised. The hearers would never have experienced or imagined such love.

The young man wastes no time in leaving. He would need to, given the nature of the extended family, and village community solidarity. The villagers, especially if approached concerning the sale, would be amazed and horrified. A family estate is part of personal identity. The son incurs their loathing and displeasure. He is also radically breaking off relationship with his community.

One aspect of the story which often passes unnoticed is the presence of the older brother. The father 'divided his estate between them'. The older brother ought to have refused his share in protest at the implications of his brother's request; but he remains silent (and benefits from the transaction). Perhaps his relationship with his father is not all that it should be. Furthermore, oriental culture would expect him to adopt the role of reconciler, and he neglects/refuses to do so, even for his father's sake. The final scene of the parable makes a lot more sense when we recognise the state of relationships at the outset! It is clear that the brothers don't get on, and would not 'dwell together'.

Far country

So the young man sets off for a far country, for the diaspora, to enjoy what the world has to offer. There he has a riotous time, quickly squandering his money. (The text does not imply the later innuendo of his brother that he wastes his money in an immoral way of life.) He was carefree and dissipated, simply. Eventually, he finds himself penniless and friendless in a land racked by famine. As an outsider at such a distressing time he was particularly vulnerable. His only means of survival is to hire himself out to a gentile landowner. (The verb is 'glue himself', really hanging on.) Normally, the way to get rid of such an unwanted person is to assign him a job which he would refuse. So he is sent to mind the pigs, the most degrading occupation a Jew could engage in. He is thus working for gentiles, dealing with unclean animals, unable to observe the sabbath, and so is, for all practical purposes, outside his religion, the epitome of lostness. On top of that, he isn't getting enough to eat, and can't make up the deficit with the bitter, unnourishing wild carobs. He is starving to death.

So he thinks of home and decides to return. His 'coming to his senses' isn't really repentance, initially. It's simply that he has come to the end of his tether and is motivated by hunger. But then he does seem prepared to admit that he has done wrong (before heaven and in the sight of his father) by squandering the money which he ought to have kept aside to support his father in old age. He devises a plan of action to remedy that. He intends to order his father to carry it out, namely to take him on as a hired servant. Now a hired servant wasn't a slave, and didn't belong to the estate. He was employed and paid, but remained free and independent, living in the local village. His social status would not be inferior to father or brother; he could thus maintain his pride; and he could use his wages to fulfil his financial responsibilities to his father, paying him his due. (He can save himself; he wants no 'grace'.) Such a plan also means that, not having to live at home, he won't be dependent on his brother and incur his resentment; nor will he need to be reconciled. (There isn't a lot of love in all this!)

Returning to the village would be a problem. He returns as a failure. The manner of his leaving won't help – he had offended the entire community by taking and selling his inheritance while his father was alive. And he had lost all the money – to gentiles. So his return would be humiliating and hostile. That problem had to be faced.

The return

The scene changes, and the spotlight focuses on the father left behind, living in the village as part of that community. Doubtless his friends had told him often what a mistake he had made in the first place. He'd be aware of what would happen if the son were ever to return, especially if he returned as a failure (and maybe he didn't expect him to succeed!). A crowd would quickly gather, and he would be taunted and mocked and humiliated and abused.

The father's actions, when he catches sight of the young man, are calculated to protect the boy from the hostility of the village and to restore him to fellowship within the community. All that follows springs from compassion: 'his heart went out to him.' This is the key phrase in the narrative.

He runs to meet him (which is itself a humiliating thing for a nobleman or elder to do – but it makes it possible to reach him outside the village boundary). And a most remarkable reconciliation takes place. The father says nothing, but his actions express his profound love, acceptance and welcome. He kisses him again and again in a firm, manly embrace. (He is searching for his son like the shepherd and the woman in the parallel parables.) Such a kiss is a sign of forgiveness and reconciliation, and is public, for all the gathering villagers to see. Total, unexpected, loving acceptance. And now no one will deny him acceptance.

The son, utterly overwhelmed, begins to blurt out his oft-rehearsed confession plan. But he doesn't say, 'Make me one of your hired servants.' This is not because he is interrupted by his father shouting instructions to his servants. (He could have finished it later!) Nor is it that he, in self-interest, decides to keep quiet and accept sonship rather than hired work, because sonship has disadvantages: he would be under his father's authority and have to live with his brother, and wouldn't have the satisfaction of earning his own way. No, now he has genuinely 'come to his senses' and repented. He realises that it isn't a question of lost money but a broken relationship which he cannot heal. The possibility of a new relationship can only come as a pure gift from the father. This gift is on offer. He can accept graciousness . . . 'I am not worthy . . .' The father's compassionate love has changed him, and this is repentance.

Then the father interrupts, and begins to issue orders to the accompanying servants. They are to dress him in his father's best robe, reserved for feast days and big occasions. His wearing his father's robe at the subsequent banquet would assure his acceptance and reconciliation with servants, household and village community. The signet ring is a sign of trust. The shoes show that he is a free man in his house, and ensure the respect of the servants. The father then orders the killing of the fatted calf, indicating that the whole village community would be invited to the banquet to share their joy. An enormous celebration is envisaged. The father is paying the son an extraordinary honour.

There are no recriminations, no lecture, no reference to what has happened; his disgrace is blotted out, engulfed in a flood-tide of loving mercy. And he accepts this grace, this gift. A son is found. Father and son rejoice, and draw the whole community into the rejoicing.

Older son

Our attention is now switched to the older brother and the father's dealing with him. This section is by no means an appendix. It is entirely parallel with the previous part. And the father's response to the son is the same.

When the preparations for the feast are in full swing, the music boisterously starts up, the people begin to assemble and the men return from the fields. The older son is amongst them. On hearing the music, he realises that a celebration has started, but is suspicious; he calls on one of the many children who have congregated outside, making the most of the fun, and plies him with questions (to get maximum information). He decides not to enter. As the older son, custom demanded his presence in the role of major-domo, ensuring the well-being of all the guests. He is expected to welcome his brother and show him special attention as the honoured guest. (And then, when all is over, complain about what has happened, if he wishes!) What he does is quarrel publicly with his father, adding this insult to that of non-participation. The break between father and son is almost as radical as that much earlier between the father and the other son.

The father's response is not one of anger and displeasure; again he comes out of the house in humility and love, in order to entreat and reconcile; he comes in search of his son. The son's response is devastatingly sad. He complains, he neglects to address his father with his title. He evinces the attitude of a slave – he has been living with a 'trade union' mentality rather than that of a son at home. He claims never to have disobeyed; he is so self-righteous – yet there is no love and respect, and he has just insulted him. His estrangement and rebellion are no less real than that of his younger brother. Whilst in the house he was just as far away as his younger brother in his pigsty. He childishly accuses his father of favouritism in never even giving him a goat. He declares that he isn't part of the family – he won't even acknowledge his brother; and his desire for a party with his cronies excludes father and brother and their guests – his community is elsewhere. He won't rejoice here. And then he goes on in his antipathy to put a bad interpretation on his brother's conduct. (He may even be attempting to demonstrate that his brother is a rebellious son and therefore worthy of death!) Bitterness, arrogance, insult, distortion of facts, unjust accusations.

And how does the father respond? Again there is no anger, no judgement or criticism; again just an outpouring of love and compassion. As he reaches out in search, to bridge the gap, he begins with a title of deep affection, welling from a heart pained by rejection and longing to see his two sons together again in his house. With gentleness and patience he appeals to him to rejoice in his brother's return. He lays to rest any fears about his own inheritance, for 'everything I have is yours', his rights are secure and fully protected. He is the heir. (Actually, the implication is that the older son, who has owned everything since his brother left, is angry that he can't dispose of it, even for a party; it would be better for him if his father died . . . !)

The father gently tries to remind his son that the cause of the celebration is the return of his brother; he is appealing for him to understand his loving compassion and free forgiveness. It is an attempt to lead him into freedom, fellowship and festivity.

The father wants sons. The younger son was dead and is now alive. The older son is dead. And we are left, tantalisingly unsure whether he accepted the offer of life.

Rev Michael Winstanley SDB

I would like to express my indebtedness to K. E. Bailey, *Poet and Peasant* and *Through Peasant Eyes* (Grand Rapids, Eerdmans, 1983) for many insights into this parable.

Celebrating Reconciliation

I am loved

Welcome

I am a child of God.
God loves me.
I am baptised in the family of the Church.

Listen

I am quiet and still.
I listen to Jesus speaking . . .
the lost son, the lost sheep,
the lost coin, the little man.

Remember

I look back and think about my life.
I remember the times when I haven't loved,
haven't shared, haven't cared.

Rejoice

1 I say hello
2 I talk about my life
3 I tell God I'm sorry
4 I promise to love and try again
5 I listen to the words of God's forgiveness
6 I say goodbye and thank you

Thank

I give thanks that I am loved and forgiven.

Sr Catherine Darby SND

We celebrate forgiveness with others
(Communal Rite of Reconciliation – Rite 2)

At times we celebrate the Sacrament of Reconciliation with the priest and with other people in our parish. This rite helps us say we are sorry and reminds us of how Christ lived.

- We gather as the family of God. We may sing a hymn. The priest welcomes us and says the opening prayer.
- We listen to a story from the Bible about God's love and forgiveness.
- We remember that God always loves us and forgives us when we are sorry for our sins.
- We think about the way we have lived.
- We say we are sorry together in an Act of Contrition.
- We pray the Lord's Prayer.
- The priest meets us one by one.
  (You tell your sins to the priest.
  You say you are sorry and promise to do better.
  The priest gives you a penance.
  The priest absolves you in the name of God and the Church.)
- We give thanks and praise for God's mercy and loving forgiveness.
- We are blessed.
- We are asked to bring Jesus' peace to others.
- We pray or sing to thank God.

(This structure may vary depending on the way your parish normally celebrates Rite 2.)

Guidelines for children
celebrating the Sacrament of Reconciliation

1. Kneel down and talk to God our Father about why you have come to the sacrament and think about what you want to tell the priest. Remember just two or three things you are sorry you did or you could have done better.

2. When it is your turn to talk to the priest make the sign of the Cross with him, and listen to what he says. Then tell him about the times you did not behave as Jesus would have liked you to.

3. The priest will then talk to you and ask you to say a prayer or do something to show you are really sorry. This is your 'penance'.

4. He will then ask you to say your 'Sorry' prayer and he will say the words of forgiveness.

5. When he says you may go, say 'Thank you, Father.' You can then kneel in church, and say 'Thank you' to God our Father for loving you and giving you Jesus to help you.

My Book About Forgiveness
J. H. Stratton
Aids for RE

APPENDIX

Resources for prayer

Readings

Session 1
'Speak to Us of Children', Kahlil Gibran
from *The Prophet,*
William Heinemann Ltd. First published 1926
(see page 120)

Session 2
Dramatised 'Our Father'
source unknown
(see pages 121-123)

Session 3
'I'm Not that Kind of God', M. Quinn
from *How to Prepare your Child for the Sacrament of Penance*
Veritas Family Resources
(see page 124)

Session 4
The Prodigal Son, Luke 15:11-32 (see pages 106-107)
or Ephesians 3:14-21 (see page 125)

Hymns

The numbers refer to *Hymns Old and New with Supplement* (HON) and to *Liturgical Hymns Old and New* (LITON), both published by Kevin Mayhew Ltd.

Session 1
'The Lord's my Shepherd', HON 534, LITON 661

Session 2
'Yahweh, I know you are near', HON 620, LITON 744

Session 3
'I will never forget you, my people', HON 265, LITON 382
'Be still and know that I am God', HON 58, LITON 164

Session 4
'God forgave my sin in Jesus' name', HON 175, LITON 286
'O, the love of my Lord is the essence', HON 430, LITON 557

Closing prayers – See page 126

Blessings – See page 126

Speak to us of children

And a woman who held a babe against her bosom said,
'Speak to us of children'.
And he said:
'Your children are not your children.
They are the sons and daughters of Life's longing for itself.
They come through you but not from you,
and though they are with you yet they belong not to you.

You may give them your love but not your thoughts,
for they have their own thoughts.
You may house their bodies but not their souls,
for their souls dwell in the house of tomorrow,
which you cannot visit, not even in your dreams.
You may strive to be like them,
but seek not to make them like you.
For life goes not backward nor tarries with yesterday.
You are the bows from which your children as living arrows are sent
    forth.
The archer sees the mark upon the path of the infinite, and he
bends you with his might that his arrows may go swift and far.
Let your bending in the Archer's hand be for gladness;
for even as he loves the arrow that flies,
so he loves also the bow that is stable.

The Prophet
Kahlil Gibran
William Heinemann Ltd

The Lord's Prayer dramatised

P Our Father who art in heaven . . .

G Yes? . . .

P Don't interrupt me, I'm praying.

G But you called.

P Did I? I didn't call you, I'm praying. Our Father who art in heaven . . .

G There, you did it again.

P Did what?

G Called me. You said, 'Our Father who art in heaven'. Here I am. What's on your mind?

P But I didn't mean anything by it. I was, you know, just saying my prayers for the day. I always say the Lord's Prayer. It makes me feel good, sort of like getting the job done.

G All right, go on.

P Hallowed be thy name . . .

G Hold it, what do you mean by that?

P By what?

G By 'Hallowed be thy name'?

P It means . . . it means . . . well, I don't know what it means. How should I know? It's just part of the prayer. By the way, what does it mean?

G It means holy, honoured, wonderful.

P Ah, that makes sense. I never thought about what 'Hallowed' meant before. Thy kingdom come, thy will be done, on earth as it is in heaven . . .

G Do you really mean that?

P Of course, why not?

G Well what are you going to do about it then?

P Do? Nothing, I suppose. I just think it would be rather good if you got control of everything down here as you have up there.

G Have I got control of you?

P Well, I go to church.

G That isn't what I asked you. What about your habit of lying? And your bad temper? You've really got a problem there, you know. And then there's the way you spend your money . . . all on yourself. And what about the kind of books you read?

P Stop picking on me! *I'm* just as good as the other lot down there at church!

G Excuse me. I thought you were praying for my will to be done. If that is to happen then it will have to start with the ones who are praying for it. Like you . . .

121

P   Oh, all right. I guess I do have some faults. Now you come to mention it, I could probably name some others.

G   So could I.

P   I haven't thought about it very much until now, but I really would like to cut out some of these things. I would like to be really free.

G   Good, now we're getting somewhere. We'll work together. You and me. Some victories can truly be won, I'm proud of you.

P   Look, Lord, I need to get this finished. It's taking a lot longer than it usually does. Give us this day our daily bread . . .

G   You need to cut the bread out, you're overweight as it is.

P   Hey, what is this? Criticise-me day? Here I was doing my religious duty and you suddenly butt in and remind me of all my hang-ups.

G   Praying is a dangerous thing you know, you could end up being changed! That's what I'm trying to get across to you. You called me and here I am. It's too late to stop now. Keep on praying. I'm interested in the next part of your prayer . . . *(pause)* . . . Well, go on.

P   I'm scared.

G   Scared . . . of what?

P   I know what you'll say.

G   Try me and see.

P   Forgive us our trespasses as we forgive those who trespass against us . . .

G   What about Bill?

P   See, I knew it! I knew you would bring him up! Why, Lord, he's told so many lies about me, cheated me out of money. He never paid back the debt he owed me. I've sworn to get even with him.

G   But your prayer, what about your prayer?

P   I didn't mean it.

G   Well, at least you're honest. But it's not much fun carrying that load of bitterness around inside, is it?

P   No, but I'll feel better as soon as I get even.

G   You won't feel any better. You'll feel worse. Revenge isn't sweet. Think of how unhappy you are already. But I can change all that. Forgive Bill. Then I'll forgive you.

P   But Lord, I can't forgive Bill.

G   Then I can't forgive you.

P   Oh! You're right. You always are. And more than I want revenge on Bill, I want to be right with you. *(pause)* . . . *(sigh)* . . . All right. I forgive him.

G   There now . . . wonderful. How do you feel?

P   Hmmm . . . well, not bad, not bad at all. In fact I feel quite tremendous.

G   You haven't finished your prayer, go on.

P   Oh! All right. And lead us not into temptation, but deliver us from evil . . .

G   Good, good . . . I'll do just that. But don't put yourself in a position where you can be tempted . . . Go ahead and finish your prayer.

P   For the kingdom, the power and the glory are yours, now and for ever. Amen.

G   Do you know what would bring me glory? What would really make me happy?

P   No. But I would like to know. I want to please you. Now I can see how good it would be to be a real follower of you.

G   *You've* just answered the question.

P   I did?

G   Yes, the thing that would bring me glory is to have you and others like you, who truly love and follow me. And I see that happening between us. Now that some of these faults are exposed and out of the way, there is no telling what we can do together.

P   Lord, let's see what we can make of me . . . OK?

G   Yes, let's see . . .

Source unknown

'I'm not that kind of God'
Clearing up a few misunderstandings about God

Some people see me as an angry judge. Some see me as a distant, bearded God. Some see me as a father, but inspiring fear like fathers they've known. So let me put the record straight for you. I'm none of these.

See me instead as I am – as gentle and encouraging as any father or any mother you could possibly imagine. I love my children dearly. All of them. Though I've a special love for those who need me more, who know how poor they are, how they have sinned and how they need forgiveness. That's only natural – aren't you the same with your own child who's ill? My heart goes out to everyone who's poor and childlike. And that's how I love you.

I love you as you are. Don't ever ask if God is pleased with you. Of course I'm pleased with you. My love has no conditions. It's not the kind of love that waits until you're 'good' or worthy. Your name is written on my very palm. You see yourself as mean and nasty, greedy, selfish, difficult to love. But I don't see you that way. I'll say it again. I love you as you are. As you yourself accept and love a child and find delight in her. But much more. So don't be asking if I'm pleased with you. Ask yourself instead if you've remembered that you're my growing child, that those around you are my children too, your brothers and your sisters. That's a helpful and a central question.

You think of me as God almighty, with a memory that stores up all your sins until the final judgement. But I forget your sins so quickly. I forgive and I forget. I always see you new and fresh and starting on a new beginning. I know you've sinned, of course – but that just makes me open wide my arms and think: 'My child, you're far more dear and more important to me than anything you did.' As long as you believe I love you, nothing can come between us. As long as you remember you're the child of a forgiving God.

You know something? I never even punish sin. I'm not that kind of parent. Sin punishes itself. Its consequences hurt. You make your own hell here on earth when you reject my open hands, when you refuse the gift of my forgiveness. But I don't punish. I'm a God who loves and saves and gives you life in all its fullness. Remember that. And remember you're my child. When that sinks in – when you can see that you're the precious child of a forgiving, loving God – you've grasped the very heart of the good news my Son has come to bring.

Another thing that you've misunderstood is sin itself. Don't think of sin as simply breaking laws. Sin is about you and me. It's all about forgetting you're my child – turning your back on me, going your own way and refusing to turn back.

You know what it's like when your own child is cold and distant. In the same way it breaks my heart to see you drift along unthinking and unconscious of my love. But when you turn back to me and really want to make amends, when you're sorry for the damage done to your sisters and your brothers and you wonder how to make it up to them, when you confess humbly and admit your selfishness, then I come running down the road to meet you. My love and forgiveness can touch you once again, and in heaven there is joy and celebration.

So remember who you are. And that I love you and will always be with you.

How to Prepare Your Child for the Sacrament of Penance, Veritas Family Resources
Dublin, 1985

Ephesians 3:14-21

For this reason I bow my knees before the Father, from whom every family in heaven and on earth takes its name. I pray that, according to the riches of his glory, he may grant that you may be strengthened in your inner being with power through his Spirit, and that Christ may dwell in your hearts through faith, as you are being rooted and grounded in love. I pray that you may have the power to comprehend, with all the saints, what is the breadth and length and height and depth, and to know the love of Christ that surpasses knowledge, so that you may be filled with all the fullness of God.

Now to him who by the power at work within us is able to accomplish abundantly far more than all we can ask or imagine, to him be glory in the church and in Christ Jesus to all generations, for ever and ever. Amen.

NRSV

Closing prayers

1.

Glory be to the Father and to the Son
and to the Holy Spirit . . .

Traditional

2.

Enable us, Father, Creator,
to walk in your light,
to work by your might,
to long for your sight.

Enable us, Jesus, Redeemer,
to look for your healing,
to know your appealing,
to live for your revealing.

Enable us, Spirit, Strengthener,
with power through your confiding,
with peace through your providing,
with Presence through your abiding.

Enable us,
Trinity
in Unity,
Unity
in Trinity.
Enable us, O God.

Power Lines
David Adam
Triangle Press, SPCK, 1992

3.

O Christ,
tirelessly you seek out those who are
looking for you
and who think that you are far away;
teach us, at every moment,
to place our spirits in your hands.
While we are still looking for you,
already you have found us.
However poor our prayer,
you hear us far more than we can
imagine or believe.

Praying Together in Word and Song
Taizé, Mowbray 1989

4.

Deep peace of the running wave to you,
deep peace of the flowing air to you,
deep peace of the quiet earth to you,
deep peace of the shining stars to you,
deep peace of the Son of peace to you.
Amen.

Celtic prayer

Blessings

1.

The grace of our Lord Jesus Christ,
the love of God
and the fellowship of the Holy Spirit
be with all this night
and always. Amen.

2.

May the peace of God which is
beyond all understanding
keep our hearts and minds in the
knowledge and love of God
and of his Son our Lord Jesus Christ.
And may almighty God bless us,
the Father, the Son and the Holy
Spirit. Amen.

3.

The blessing of God of life be ours,
the blessing of the loving Christ be ours,
the blessing of the Holy Spirit be ours,
to cherish us, to help, to make us holy.
Amen.

Worship Book
The Iona Community
Wild Goose Publication, 1991

4.

May the Lord bless us and keep us
from all evil and bring us to everlasting
life. Amen.

Recommended reading

For deepening your own understanding of Reconciliation

Reconciliation for the Millennium
Bishops' Conference of England and Wales
Catholic Truth Society, 1999

A Parish Pastoral Directory, chapter 4
Ed. William Dalton. The Columba Press, 1995

'Reconciliation', chapter 8, Patrick Purnell SJ
from *The Candles Are Still Burning*
Ed. Mary Grey. Geoffrey Chapman, 1995.

Rethinking Sacraments: Holy Moments in Daily Living, Bill Huebsch
Twenty-Third Publications. Fifth Printing, 1995

Sacraments Revisited, chapter 6, Liam Kelly
Darton, Longman & Todd Ltd, 1998

The Return of the Prodigal Son, Henri Nouwen
Darton, Longman & Todd, 1994

The Gift of Forgiveness
Gerald O'Mahony SJ
CTS, 1981

Focus on the Sacraments, Peter Wilkinson
Kevin Mayhew Ltd, 1987

Catechism of the Catholic Church: Part 2
Section 2, chapter 2, article 4
Geoffrey Chapman, 1994

How to Survive Being Married to a Catholic,
Redemptorist Publications, 1986

Your Child's First Confession
Redemptorist Publications, 1993

So Much to Celebrate, Tony Castle
Kevin Mayhew Ltd, 2000

Celebrating with Children, Sister Joan Brown
Kevin Mayhew Ltd, 1999

Acknowledgements

The publishers wish to express their gratitude to the following for permission to include copyright material in this publication:

Bernard Bickers.

Bloodaxe Books, PO Box 1SN, Newcastle upon Tyne, NE99 1SN, for the extracts from *A Time for Voices: Selected Poems 1960-1990* by Brendan Kennelly (Bloodaxe Books, 1990).

Ruth Cardwell.

The Catholic Truth Society, 40-46 Harleyford Road, Vauxhall, London, SE11 5AY, for the extracts from *Christifideles Laici* and *The Pope Teaches – The Pope in Britain*.

The Continuum International Publishing Group Ltd, Wellington House, 125 Strand, London, WC2R 0BB, for the extracts from *Catechism of the Catholic Church* and *Listen to Love* by Louis Savary *et al*, and *Praying Together in Word and Song*.

Sr Catherine Darby SND.

Darton, Longman & Todd, 1 Spencer Court, 140-142 Wandsworth High Street, London, SW18 4JJ, for the extracts from *Letting Go in Love* by John Dalrymple, published and © 1986 Darton, Longman & Todd Ltd. Bible quotations taken from the *Jerusalem Bible*, published and copyright 1966, 1967 and 1968 by Darton, Longman & Todd Ltd, and Doubleday & Co. Inc. *God of Surprises* by Gerard W. Hughes, published and © 1985 and 1996 Darton, Longman & Todd Ltd, and *The Return of the Prodigal Son* by Henri J. M. Nouwen, published and © 1992 Darton, Longman & Todd.

Gill & Macmillan, Goldenbridge, Dublin 8, Ireland, for the extract from *Prayers of Life* by Michael Quoist, Gill & MacMillan, 1963.

The Grail (England), c/o Lesley Toll, 23 Carlisle Road, London, NW6 6TL, for Psalm 138, taken from *The Psalms – The Grail Translations*.

International Commission on English in the Liturgy, 1522 K Street, N.W., Suite 1000, Washington DC, 20005-1202, USA, for the excerpts from the English translation of *The Roman Missal* © 1973, International Committee on English in the Liturgy, Inc. (ICEL), excerpts from the English translation of *Rite of Penance* © 1974 ICEL; excerpts from the English translation of *Eucharistic Prayers for Masses of Reconciliation* © 1975 ICEL. All rights reserved.

The Iona Community, 840 Govan Road, Glasgow, G51 3UT, for *The Blessing* from 'Carmina Gaedelica', adapted by Katy Galloway in *The Iona Community Worship Book* (Wild Goose Publications, 1991).

Mercier Press, PO Box 5, 5 French Street, Cork, Ireland, for the extract from *The Prophet*, by David Torkington.

Liturgy Training Publications, 1800 North Hermitage Avenue, Chicago, IL 60622-1101, USA, for the illustrations by Steve Erspamer, taken from the *Clipart* series: A, B, C, © 1992, 1993, 1994, Archdiocese of Chicago: Liturgy Training Publications, 1-800-933-1800. All rights reserved. Used by permission.

The National Committee for Gibran, New York, for the extract from *The Prophet*, by Kahlil Gibran, published by William Heinemann Ltd, 1926.

SCM Press, 9-17 St Albans Place, London, N1 0NX, for the extract from *Christianity Rediscovered* by Vincent Donovan, SCM Press, 1978.

SPCK Publishing, Holy Trinity Church, Marylebone Road, London, NW1 4DU, for the extract from *Power Lines* by David Adam.

St Joseph's Pastoral Centre, St Joseph's Grove, The Burroughs, Hendon, London, NW4 4TY, for the extract by Rosemary McCloskey and June Edwards, © the authors, St Joseph's Pastoral Centre, Diocese of Westminster.

St Pauls Publishing, 187 Battersea Bridge Road, London, SW11 3AS, for the extract from *To God with Love and Sorrow* by Brentwood Religious Education Service, St Pauls (UK), 1992.

J.H. Stratton.

Veritas Publications, 7-8 Lower Abbey Street, Dublin 1, Ireland, for the extract from *How to Prepare your Child for the Sacrament of Penance*, first published and © by Veritas Family Resources.

Rev Michael Winstanley SDB.

Every effort has been made to trace the owners of copyright material and we hope that no copyright has been infringed. Pardon is sought and apology made if the contrary be the case, and a correction will be made in any reprint of this book.